# My Landlord Helper

**KEYS TO MANAGING YOUR REAL ESTATE INVESTMENTS, ACHIEVING EXPLOSIVE GROWTH and SAVING MONEY**

by

Linda Liberatore

Published by Best Seller Publishing®, Pasadena, CA
Best Seller Publishing® is a registered trademark
Printed in the United States of America.
ISBN-13: 978-1545031360
ISBN-10: 1545031363

This publication is designed to provide accurate and authoritative information with regard to the subject matter covered. It is sold with the understanding that the publisher is not engaged in rendering legal, accounting, or other professional advice. If legal advice or other expert assistance is required, the services of a competent professional should be sought. The opinions expressed by the authors in this book are not endorsed by Best Seller Publishing® and are the sole responsibility of the author rendering the opinion.

Most Best Seller Publishing® titles are available at special quantity discounts for bulk purchases for sales promotions, premiums, fundraising, and educational use. Special versions or book excerpts can also be created to fit specific needs.

For more information, please write:

Best Seller Publishing®
1346 Walnut Street, #205
Pasadena, CA 91106
or call 1(626) 765 9750
Toll Free: 1(844) 850-3500

Visit us online at: www.BestSellerPublishing.org

# Dedication

I dedicate this book to my husband Tim and
my daughters Marissa, Jenna and Karli.

You are always in my heart and give me the inspiration
each day to work just a little harder.

# Foreword

This book is more than just a blueprint for growing your property portfolio. It's creative exposure to strategies and tactics that will increase your cash flow and net worth.

This book brings a positively bold approach by reinforcing a vital aspect any real estate entrepreneur can learn, which is growth. So frequently, we get caught up in the daily grind, and we fail to notice key resources right at our fingertips. And fail to be bold enough to take the next step! In real estate, we all thirst for growth in our portfolios, but the path to get there can be daunting. For growth to occur, there are many components that must form. One such factor is knowledge. Seeking out the most important resources to elevate our growth takes persistence, and Linda has the expertise and blueprint to find that growth.

We must not only be able to seek out the tools to achieve growth, but know how to implement them in order to make an impact. I've seen that unfold with my real estate career after doing a successful daily podcast episode for over two years. Taking the risk to expand your resources outside of the original box is crucial. Momentum builds and opportunities blossom from the energy of growth. But you must have a blueprint to get there.

Something else this book does is creatively build the necessary platform that directly correlates to your real estate investing success. There's always an opportunity for growth, and a consistent effort to not only recognize but to implement those resources is a gateway to success.

So, take this book in and soak up each of the chapters. From educating yourself on the key pieces to have in place, to how to manage growth and everything in between, this book has the necessary information every real estate investor should know.

— Joe Fairless

Author of *Best Real Estate Investing Advice Ever: Volume 1*

# Personal Story

How did I get here today, and what brought me to this book? An intense passion to deliver on my commitments. When I say I'm going to do something, I do it. So, when I started this business, I began to reach out to real estate investors and learned quickly that many of these investors found themselves in difficult financial positions when tenants were slow to pay.

I'd hear that yes, there was a legal process, but it wasn't a process people relished or would go through. The average new investor would just say, "Oh, shouldn't the legal process take care of it?" But in listening to the stories, the law wasn't taking care of it. This put them in a very difficult situation.

This is a very people-based business. When you place some type of service in that position, whether it is My Landlord Helper or somebody else, you quickly start to see the value that it offers. In my case, I quickly saw the value of my passion for trying to correct this problem. It was very difficult, though. I felt a lot of empathy towards the people who were in these situations. I saw how difficult it was for them to scale when they were in a smaller position, and it became a heartfelt thing to be making these kinds of decisions when it came to the money. I reflected and realized that with my background, knowledge of the technology, and the people situation, I had the ability to help others.

The "helper" tag came naturally to me because that's the all-in passion that I bring to a project. When anyone has ever asked me, "Can you help me solve this problem?" whether it be man-hours or technology or just sitting and listening, I have arisen to the situation. Helping has always been my calling.

In addition to what I've learned over the years, I believe that business is in my blood. Growing up I studied my dad, who was a successful businessman for many years. He was also a millionaire in social capital. He always had the time to share a story or lend a hand for anyone who crossed his path.

I was destined for this journey and am excited to share my learnings with you.

# Introduction

You may be wondering, *What is a landlord helper?* If you've picked up this book, you probably own real estate investment properties and may want to expand your portfolio, or you're considering your first property purchase. If you're looking to expand, investment properties require trial, error, a daily commitment, and lots of heavy lifting; it's no different from any small business. Landlord helpers make it possible for owners like you to do just that.

In my many years of working with investors, I've seen too many high-energy, passionate self-starters seek the help of my office. They come to us filled with stress and fear about jumping into the real estate business without a plan. They also seek guidance when their current process becomes too burdensome and they are starting to lose the vision of their future. If you're seriously committed to growing a portfolio, at some point you'll need help.

My mission with this book is to empower both new and experienced landlords to examine your current situation and determine what is working and where you require assistance. Establishing this baseline will set the stage for you to move forward with purchasing additional properties. Whatever your goal and however many doors you have envisioned in your future, you must enable yourself to move forward.

Landlord helpers, including my business, *My Landlord Helper*, make it possible for you to outsource the simplest of tasks to save you time and money. Our clients praise us for enabling them to keep control of their cash and minimize their expenses. Just as with a small business, when you begin the journey you soon find out how quickly money begins to go out. Until your properties are paid off, the margins are pretty thin and additional cash flow can be limited.

This book is based on many stories and experiences with landlords across the nation who found the assistance they needed to grow their current portfolio tenfold, and how I helped them through my company. There are no shortcuts to success, however, so I discuss various methods and approaches to maximizing your time, operations, and mindset throughout the book.

Prior to forming *My Landlord Helper*, I had been working in small businesses for over 20 years. It was in this role that I realized the opportunity and need for real estate investors to have better support so they can focus on the bottom line and not minute details.

In my many years leading *My Landlord Helper*, I have watched the positive impact transition development has had on our clients and the plentiful rewards they have received. Avoiding foreclosure, increasing their occupancy rates, bringing structure to their collections, and simplifying the maintenance process are just a few examples. This book exists today because of the many instances I've witnessed where the outcomes weren't so positive. I am excited to share this knowledge with you so you too can implement proven strategies to save you time and money!

# Table of Contents

# CHAPTER 1

# Boost Your Portfolio

When you get comfortable with the thought of partnering with a helper, your world and your vision for growth expands. You realize you can develop a plan to follow the real estate investing masterminds and purchase additional properties. One of the key plans is buying a couple of properties a year and developing a roadmap to have the property paid off in seven to ten years. Growing equity will happen simultaneously as you continue to target more properties that will support your goal of boosting your portfolio.

Creating a proper financial strategy paves the way for your portfolio to launch to the next level. Always keep this in mind, especially when buying your first property. Remember that the mortgage, real estate taxes, and many expenses must be deducted from the income that's produced by the rent and may leave you with a slim profit. Thus, building a portfolio that's based on early payoff sees you in a much more liquid position, much quicker.

The current economic state is in your favor. As a landlord, you benefit from the fact that rents are at a record high, which produces the highest possible rent return. On the income side, interest rates being at an all-time low allows you the benefit of being able to apply additional funds you're saving in interest to the principal balance, thus paying off your loans quicker. That prepares you for the cycle of when rates begin to climb and rents start to stabilize.

# SENIOR PROPERTIES

My company works with some investors who clearly focus on what we refer to as senior properties. There are many properties across the United States that were developed at a time where there were many young families filling new subdivisions. The families eventually grow, the children are off to college or married, and the parents are now empty nesters.

When you're able to identify a senior neighborhood, you'll often find that one spouse has passed and the other now lives alone in the home. In multi-family buildings, often these widows become landlords. And after a while, it is common for them to no longer be comfortable with having that responsibility.

They're fearful. Or perhaps the practice and responsibilities intimidate and overwhelm them. Sometimes they'll be willing to hold a mortgage for someone else to buy their building, take over that maintenance, and take over that responsibility of landlording. The senior may elect to remain in their unit and they want that unit to remain their home until they're no longer able to live independently. These are key opportunities for investors and are mutually beneficial, as they're helping the seniors by allowing them to live a happy, peaceful life in their original home and provide many avenues to fostering other win-win scenarios.

# PROBATE PROPERTIES

While some clients exclusively seek senior properties, others want probate properties, another major strategy. A property is classified as a probate when a homeowner has died and it now transfers as outlined in their will. What's great is that seniors often take great pride in caring for their home, so their properties are generally in good condition. This makes for a great investment strategy, because the average person who is going looking to buy their first home is not looking for something out of date. They want stainless steel appliances, ceramic floors, marble counter tops and the like.

Probate homes don't offer that appeal, but an investor will appreciate that the foundation, structure, and roof are solid. They simply have to make cosmetic repairs; it is an ideal situation. This can generally be done relatively inexpensively, which should immediately make the property more attractive to potential renters.

Sometimes, however, probate situations can be very sensitive for the obvious reason that there has been a recent death in the family. During this time, family members in receipt of the property are also evaluating what they want to do with the estate that's been left to them. If they decide to sell by listing on the multiple listing service (MLS), the real estate agent generally advises them to begin to pursue repairs and upgrades. However, once they see that they must use out-of-pocket money upfront to do that, they're much more receptive to an offer from an investor who is saying, "I'll take it *as is* for this lower amount." This relieves the family of their headache and you now have a new property added to your portfolio. It is another win-win scenario.

So how do you best position yourself to buy a probate property? Presence and timing. There are marketing companies that specifically provide lists of which properties are in probate. With this information, you're then able to develop a mail campaign that you'll send to the family who inherited the property you're interested in. By doing this regularly (I recommend monthly), you're creating name recognition and serving as a potential solution to this new concern of theirs. This approach has proven successful for many of my clients.

## MLS SEARCH

Another strategy to find great investment properties is to simply review the MLS daily. This should include not only brand-new listings but also expired listings. The key is to set up filters and/or search agents that pinpoint exact details of the type of home you're seeking. Once the criteria are set, it can be exported and further manipulated to determine actual value based on costs and considerations. From there, you can determine if the property should be a rental and evaluate the rental market in that area.

Lastly is what I call "a ring of the bell." Based on your data, you may put 20 offers out per week. Some do this on a regular basis and make the offers as often and low as possible, ending up generally with at least three properties. This is another great tactic to grow your portfolio!

If you speak to any successful investor, they have a price range and targets in mind. And since you'd be unable to visit hundreds of properties per week and you want to save money by not hiring someone, the only way to seriously and effectively evaluate all opportunities is through the review you'll do with the information you've exported. One great tool for evaluating potential rehab properties is Rehab Valuator, which is available online. If you join a REIA or community such as biggerpockets.com you will find calculators for rentals, flips, and wholesaling. One popular calculator is Buy, Rehab, Rent, Refinance, Repeat. This strategy will not only grow your portfolio but also create efficiency in your search practices. Any time you can comparison shop by using proven tools it will assist you in zoning in on your perfect property.

## SELF-DIRECTED IRA

One investor that I work with who is based on the west coast takes her IRA assets and turns those into a self-directed IRA. You may not be familiar with this concept, so let's define it. Wikipedia defines a self-directed Individual Retirement Account as an Individual Retirement Account (IRA) provided by some financial institutions in the United States which allow alternative investments for retirement savings.

When you take a self-directed IRA, it allows you to take tax-free retirement funds and purchase real estate investments. The IRS is essentially allowing you to do just as you would with a money market account. There are of course many laws that go with this, just as there are many laws regulating IRA accounts.

There are advisors who can guide you on setting this up and ensure that those tax laws are benefiting you. I say "benefiting you" because that changes according to your scenario: where you are in life, how old you are, and what type of investments you want to use. See a successful tax advisor who is familiar with this, not just a general accountant.

In current economic times, any money that's in an IRA probably isn't yielding you the best investment returns. Real estate transactions, however, have multiple benefits. Not only is the rate of return higher, but so are the additional tax laws and write-offs that you can use.

While foreclosures have gone down each year, there are still, and always will be, a number of homes that people lose to the banks each day for nonpayment. When this happens, banks generally look to get these properties off their books. Banks do not want to become landlords; they would prefer more favorable cash assets on their balance sheet. These bank-owned properties go to local auctions. Many of our investors have built a great track record by working closely with banks, which results in banks letting these investors know when new properties are becoming available.

Most commonly, those interested in foreclosures will attend their local county auction. Once you've focused on one county, you start to anticipate what will become available. Generally, these auctions are held each week. You'll know the stack from the previous week that hasn't been sold off or hasn't been bid on. You'll develop a good sense of what a three-bedroom/two-bath, for example, is going for.

When I use the term "local" regarding auctions and real estate investing, it's as local as a specific block. In other words, when you take an area of your own city in your mind and you think about it, there are always stronger and weaker areas of that city. Economically there are some areas that can be challenged as well as areas that are prospering, often within one mile or seven-block radius in one square mile. Getting to know the auction, you can really pick up some great bargains. I experienced firsthand how you can get property for as low as $15,000. That same property can be worth $150,000 and be listed for sale after all the renovations, often easily clearing $50,000!

There are also often multi-family buildings at foreclosure auctions. If you're not one to wait for an opportunity, you can follow suit with other investors who specifically look for owners who have put themselves in a bad position. You can identify this type of owner when they owe too much on their investments and they are looking for an escape. In those cases, they must accept, for example, seventy cents on the dollar because of the fact that they're in a financially bad situation. These owners may have bought too many investments and they need help. One person's misfortune makes for the next investor's opportunity.

These are just a few of the many stories and experiences we've heard from our clients about how they go about finding areas of opportunity. As you can see, all of them require a great deal of effort and really being in touch with the market. Yet this is often where the conflict comes in; trying to manage an existing portfolio as they try to build their expertise in these areas of expansion is a juggling act – and they need help!

Good investors realize their value is in finding the next deal. There are thousands of dollars to be saved by becoming intimately familiar with your real estate investment target area. Hard work is the road most traveled to establish a business your path to a large real estate portfolio will be no different. Becoming a leader in your area requires establishing strong relationships with lenders, other investors, and many professionals you will need on your team. These relationships and your ability to buy property at the lowest possible price provides you with the greatest return on your money. Recognizing that you are a skilled professional requires you to allot the necessary time to explode your education and focus on the return.

CHAPTER 2

# Free Up and Save Time

Once you understand the many ways that investors add properties, you quickly realize how getting help becomes a necessity, not a luxury. The business-savvy professional will always find areas to automate and save time. The idea of automating an overlaying function so we can join it to a successful conclusion is a key to many successful business tasks. When my landlords realized the value of a service specifically set up to be their property management assistant, each lit up with excitement and experienced a wave of relief.

One of the ways my company automates is by using a process to batch and expedite payments with automated clearinghouse (ACH) tools at the bank. This process is established when the convenience of ACH payment is explained as part of onboarding a new tenant. We can accept a prescheduled payment for a specific day of the month, most often the first or a date approved by the landlord within their grace period. We also allow the convenience of an on-demand option, letting the resident call, text, email, or use our convenient tenant portal to determine the date that fits for that specific month.

By offering this variety of options, we have eliminated many excuses for late payments and meet the needs of our investors. Each payment is crucial to an investor's cash flow, so by expanding our flexibility, it ensures that we're removing hurdles and enabling the tenant to be able to pay on time.

I once had an investor, Johnny, who was offering the optimal solution for his tenants — or so he thought. They could go directly to Johnny's bank and deposit their rent. What Johnny didn't count on was the extra time it took to identify which deposit belonged to which tenant. It was a burden. He had outlined a clear procedure for the tenants to mark their deposits, but never really thought through the fact that he'd have to wait 24 hours for the bank to post the scanned copy of each deposit slip, the document which showed him which tenant had deposited the funds. This process also made it difficult to determine if customers were paying late fees since Johnny couldn't immediately get to all of the checks for cross-reference without a great amount of effort on his part.

Real estate wasn't Johnny's only profession, which made the added stress even more difficult to manage. He was in a high-pressure full-time sales job that required a large time commitment and significant focus. It became obvious to him pretty quickly that he was going to need someone to help him part time or full time. Due to the cyclical nature of the rental cycle, he decided that full time was not the best way to spend his profits. Yet it was a challenge to find anybody that could specifically do this during those five days per month when it was most critical.

Johnny sought the help of my company, Secure Pay One My Landlord Helper, and found us to be the perfect solution. We started out by sending a mail campaign to all his existing clients and new contacts, which explained the entire process of the communication that would be required to continue the convenience of going to the bank. We included bank deposit slips pre-printed with their name, included the ability to text us copies of their receipt immediately after making the deposit, and we began to educate the residents on the convenience of paying at the bank if they were to properly label their deposits. This small change led to a smoother operation for the tenant as well.

We also began an invoice campaign that showed them when payments were not paid from the previous month. This was very helpful because it allowed them to realize by not calling in a payment, there was a chance that their ledger was not getting updated until the actual bank account was reconciled. We were able to offer an extremely valuable solution, helping to quickly identify who really did need legal notices. My Landlord Helper ramped up the value of getting

Johnny's legal notices out in a quick way and of course, that allowed for the prompt identification of tenants who needed to be removed from the properties through the legal system.

Johnny has been with us now for well over two years. The onboarding process has been revamped and now both Johnny and the tenants have a more smooth and stress-free experience.

Many quick-pay solutions exist today and we ensure we offer options to make payment convenient for residents while bringing the money to our landlords as quickly as possible. We have developed a consistent system which combines reminders and invoicing. Our system includes a multi-touch reminder via text, email, and phone. Our unique color-coded mail system provides a bright visual reminder in the tenant's mind that their rent payment is due. We are complimented on the level of priority for the rent that exists for tenants after they are placed in our program. Intimately understanding the demographics of our tenants allows us to offer the customized plan that will result in effectiveness.

Since no two clients are the same, we seek to customize each client's experience when looking to meet their needs. Some investors live abroad, some specifically focus on out-of-state property, and some are new to the investment world. The common thread is that they all have a cash flow issue to an extent, whether they are starting their portfolios and each payment is needed to keep a consistent cash flow, or they are growing their portfolio and freeing up money for the next purchase. Recording and following up on rent in a timely manner can result in a very time-consuming process of keeping accurate ledgers at the beginning of each month. We offer a solution that allows landlords to stay in the director's chair, stay in control, and manage costs, all while planning the next scene.

We have clients come to us who were always behind on depositing rent checks at the bank and updating tenant ledgers. In the instant-access world we live in, this can be a very costly mistake. Many younger renters do not keep check registers or checks and may only use them for the rent. These renters are not familiar with the old concept of balancing a checkbook. New consumers log in to see if funds are available and they pay. This concept makes it a very dangerous risk to not cash checks or debit accounts on the precise date approval has been received.

Landlord helpers generally offer consulting advice and expand the automated solutions available to them for reducing redundant tasks. At *My Landlord Helper*, we make it our mission to be very tech savvy. We provide mobile and web-based options that range in cost from free to a nominal subscription charge. We work with our real estate investors to research and implement software solutions as needed to complement their process, keep them informed, and give them a slight edge. The goal is to implement a process where investors spend time in a strategy session to identify tasks that are repeated frequently, providing little value, so that they can then quickly identify what can be outsourced to save them time. Cloud-based software, such as Dropbox or Google Drive are great because they allow the convenience of making sure their information is in a shared environment where important documents can be immediately accessed from anywhere. For example, a client might inquire about researching new advantages with Zillow or Facebook marketing. They wonder what impact creating a private group might have on their community. You see more national communities posting vacancies and events to the existing residents. It also helps build a sense of strong community when residents share about events with friends in and around their buildings.

We may assist a new investor through their security deposit reconciliation statement, which can save a lot of money lost in productive time if they are not familiar with the penalties that may be imposed by their state or county. This involves working with their legal team to examine the data required by the specific county or city. Each of these statements is typically very specific to the county and state that they live in.

Most our landlords request that we handle daily direct communication with the residents. A great example of this is the move-out process. Most of our clients require a very timely move out process that may involve a new resident coming in the very next day. This move out/move in process involves a transfer of utilities and many checklists to cover specific responsibilities to orchestrate the tasks smoothly. We work with them to build that list of expectations. Once they review and finalize the steps, we capture the list of tasks and we are able to free up the landlord's time by distributing the lists during each turnover on the many units they manage.

In one large multi-family building in the City of Chicago, we assisted our client, Bob, in transforming all his existing month-to-month leases and returning each resident to an annual lease with an increase. His day-to-day tasks had increased and he was so appreciative to have our assistance with identifying resident dates and drafting new leases. Once all leases were entered into our software, the system now sends him an automated lease renewal email each week listing all upcoming lease renewals that are within 70 days of lease expiration. In the current economic environment with rents rising, this allowed him to issue small increases at renewal time that were still attractive to the resident. This helps Bob keep up with his rising costs to cover real estate taxes and other expenses. The reality for many landlords working through a growth stage is to let fewer risk-adverse tasks slip from their deadline. So, in many states and counties, if a lease expires without action by the tenant or the landlord, the lease defaults to month-to month. While it is certainly understandable that when a landlord is presented with many more pressing deadlines the lease renewal would appear the safest risk, what happens is that after losing the odd increase, the landlord will not return back to the task of updating the lease. The landlord now bears the risk of receiving a notice to vacate during non-peak months. Leases that are renewed during non-peak months often fail to be at the maximum rent in the area. Often, the unit has increased vacancy, making the options less than the most desirable.

We add a very valuable assistance when we add known efficiencies to the marketing aspect. When landlords are posting vacant or new property on the different sites that are available (Zillow, Craigslist, etc.), we will work to develop a template you'll populate each time. All that information can be saved and reused, ultimately resulting in major time saving.

This is also the case with pictures. We always suggest professional photographs. The return on investment is significant if the pictures do not represent an accurate and appealing depiction of the unit and property. There are common pictures that could be utilized in a variety of ways for all the units within your building, so they can be saved and stored appropriately. This way, when one particular unit becomes vacant, you can pull from the shared folder and we assist in quickly posting the ad.

Saving time on the preparing for the actual lease end date as it relates to marketing is also important because we're aiming to market to the next tenant before the lease expires. At least 60 days before the existing tenant has confirmed a move out date, the landlord should be prepared to circulate advertisements. This increases the probability that the new tenant moves in on the 1st, immediately after the current one departs. In a perfect world, this becomes status quo and leaves you with zero vacancies during the year.

A savvy investor realizes there is limited time in the day and once their portfolio has grown, a loss of one or two months' rent due to an ill-prepared turnover is not acceptable and may be the cause of ending the year at a loss.

Again, time is money and very precious. It is the one commodity that we cannot go out and purchase and that we cannot get back. If we can help a landlord identify the steps that save them time, they can use that time as they see fit, be it for allocating to a new purchase or more family face time.

CHAPTER 3

# Increased Productivity

One of the most common reasons that investors seek our help is to assist with tasks that help them increase their productivity in general. To best help, we ask them to really think about what their hourly rate is worth. This can aid them in seeing clearly how listing, dividing, and quantifying tasks helps clarify how to move forward in a more productive manner.

The analogy we try to give them the case of either a legal or certified public accountant (CPA) firm. These firms bill at the hourly rate of the CPA they initially speak with. In order to be most productive and cost-conscious, the firm will then evaluate the list of tasks required to serve you and delegate to the appropriate staff. This ensures that a $50 per hour employee spends time advising rather than filing paperwork, a core responsibility of the Office Manager.

Let's take a real-estate-heavy business tax return, for example. Someone with a great deal of expertise in this area is going to provide the best value and be the most productive one to make related decisions. Once the decisions are made in the respective categories, someone at the lowest level is going to be sitting with the check register to identify which checks were written by the landlord, what they were used for, and how they are to be categorized.

To increase your productivity, prior to going to the accountant you might hire somebody part-time making much less money to pre-categorize it before it gets to the accountant. Doing so would save you much time and allow you to focus on pressing needs. It would also save you money because it is being done at a fair market rate versus an accounting firm's rate.

Let's now revisit your hourly worth. This often proves to be difficult for investors to determine. Start by recalling your last minimum salary in your profession. Divide that up and use as a quantifier for each task.

One of our first clients in the far west suburbs of Chicago best captured this concept when he said, "I cannot afford to listen to phone calls from my tenants." He knew that his full-time job was dependent on commission and the task of listening to 30-minute, drama-filled messages did not have a return on investment that made it a priority duty for him. He realized that this should be outsourced and could be reduced to one actionable email. So, for him to outsource calls to us he in effect could focus on his expertise in his sales career, allowing him to continue to generate income from his properties and not lose money answering calls when his direct input was not needed.

So the first task after determining your hourly rate is to develop a list of the skill sets that make you uniquely qualified to add the most money to your bottom line.

Some of the other opportunities available for today's small rental property investment businesses are through various property management software products. While many people find them intimidating, they are extremely valuable due to the analysis they offer. They can succinctly analyze what's working and what's not, along with what's productive and what's not.

Let's envision that you're putting together your ads (as we discussed in the marketing section of the last chapter). If you use property management software, upload the pictures and upload the description, there is software that will allow you to publish the ad to many different sites at once for a nominal fee. Some software includes this by default as part of your purchased package. Occasionally, when you first use property management software, there's a lot of work up front to import your data. Keep in mind though that the long-term benefits for your productivity are huge.

If an insurance company calls you because of a claim, all that information can be queried as quickly as a Google search without the hassle of finding and sifting through papers. When you take that one incident in and of itself, you may wonder what the wage for that will equal. The real problem comes in, however, when that past gets repeated over and over and you're working your nine to five and your productivity has gone down to a zero. Yes, it requires some forethought, but that's where a landlord helper can assist you!

From a productivity standpoint, we try to help by reducing your fear of the legal cycle itself. We'll know what standard operating procedure is in your area enough to tell you where you'll want to research the specific laws pertaining to it. Take for instance the utilities notification when somebody moves in; you have the utilities change over and sometimes even register with your municipality.

We find it essential to request from your resident two additional emergency contacts at the time of move in and annually thereafter. We see inexperienced landlords not take these steps, or not have the time and resources to complete them. While an application was provided at the time of the lease start date, an annually updated emergency contact form should be required each year. Working proactively to create these types of forms helps us assist the landlord in developing the necessary move-in task checklist. You develop this checklist that can then be assigned to what I'll call, "the most inexperienced part-time help." These workers can help the owner increase their productivity by taking this checklist and verifying, "Did somebody call the utilities? Was the homeowner's association notified? Was the municipality notified of the new lease?" When you can step back and examine what the tasks are that make you more productive, you can start to clearly identify the roles that need to be outsourced at a lower level.

In one particular instance, a client allowed their tenant to move into a home prematurely because he felt it would be the most productive use of his time and get him the rent check as quickly as possible. When we use the term "prematurely," it means the home wasn't yet ready for the market. In most worlds, if you go to a property management class, they would tell you that doing so is a rookie mistake.

*Never* allow a tenant to move into a property that's not completely ready. Imagine that the rent is $1,000. While you think you might gain an extra $500 by getting them in two weeks early, what you lose in the way of risk is far greater and you now have increased the level of risk unnecessarily.

There may be safety code violations and hazards. What we try to remind owners is that sometimes neighbors that you consider trustworthy can end up reporting you; you just never know! And while yes, the city might not have time to verify each claim, neighbors worried about safety violations will follow up until resolution. Something as simple as the paint that you put on the final walls might set trigger issues with the tenant's oxygen. You just never know what type of pre-existing condition a tenant may have, and often they may not know they have a pre-existing condition. Again, you're really increasing your risk by allowing a tenant to move in pre-completion.

Additionally, the tenant may feel a sense of ownership since the lease has been signed and may want to contribute to the decisions being made. Hardwood floors versus carpeting, adding a marble countertop versus a Corian counter-top – these are your decisions to make as a landlord. Having a client move in prior to repairs and updates being completed can also lead to a web of confusion and you're opening the door for legal risk.

In one situation where a family moved in prior to work being completed, the family did feel that the home wasn't at the level they expected when repairs wrapped up. They didn't feel that the rehab was of the structure they expected. They immediately began their communication by stopping all rent payments. Yes, let me repeat: stopping all rent payments. Now we all know that legally that should never have been an option but this ended up in court after many months of back and forth and the landlord ended up losing the court case. Remember, in a court case like that, it's really going to come down to the bias of the judge. There's certainly a case to be made on both sides. The case I would make in this book is not to allow someone in the home before it's finished.

It is important to note that property management software is the most effective when you have taken the time to identify and set goals. Perhaps you want to purchase five houses this year. You don't need to be an expert on the software; you simply need to determine what factors need to be considered to make your goal a reality.

Recently, I taught a class at a local college in Illinois and there was a discussion that sometimes people try to position why their software is better than the one you're using. What you should be focusing on instead of all the features is how productive the system will make you: applicability. You must step back from the sales presentation that you heard when you selected your software. Just because the software does x, y, and z doesn't mean it's going to help you accomplish your property goals for that year.

Make sure you're always keeping track of your goals by documenting them. I suggest making a list of the most important tasks you need to accomplish once you implement the software. You'll then want to review with the sales representative which features are most commonly used. For example, templates for your application, lease, legal notices, and letters will provide you long-term savings in time and money.

A typical software implementation should be organized so there is a set date of implementation where you will cut over to the new software. To reduce the risk of errors, you should set up both systems to run concurrently for a 30-day period prior to cut off. You should validate that all contact information has been entered into the new software. The information should be checked and rechecked for accuracy. After the final payments are entered into the old software, balances must be transferred as of your target date so they can be verified for accuracy in both systems. The new system will then become your go-to system.

Getting additional temporary help on a system conversion is suggested to help things run smoothly and provide a source of checks and balances to ensure an audit trail has been set up. If your goals are to buy more property, then implementing a software solution to manage the existing property must save you time, not add hours to your day. Start simple and remember that fancy features can be mastered later on, once you've determined how to use the system to meet your goal. Discuss implementation and software support with your sales team when negotiating the purchase. If you spend weeks and weeks trying to learn all the features, but in the meantime, you didn't buy that next property, then ultimately you did not increase your productivity.

One of the many, many benefits of property management software is the recording tools. This allows you to keep track of data, which you otherwise capture with pen and paper or a spreadsheet. The ability to now read it and analyze it takes you to the next level and contributes to your productivity. We often try to work with our clients to coordinate questions the maintenance staff would like answered by creating a script specific to their needs for the office staff to use. Storing this information is a productivity time and money saver. Be sure that all resident calls and texts verify pertinent callback numbers and they are stored correctly to save time for the maintenance team. If I want to know if a particular property had a certain number of repairs, our property management maintenance report will quickly and specifically answer that question. From there you can then ask, "Is it time to examine the productivity of the maintenance person? Did that particular part or item reach its lifespan and it should be replaced? Or is this in direct correlation to a tenant behavior where the tenant behavior seems to be repeated and that might be the cause?" Having the information at your fingertips allows you to surmise the current state of the unit and evaluate trends. Again, this is a much better use of time than aggregating emails and paperwork to *hopefully* determine the accurate number of service calls made.

Ensure that you add a module that will quickly list the last date of specific quarterly or annual maintenance procedures.

Remember, however, storing data for the sake of storing does not make you more productive. We're entering an age, as a society, where we store more data than ever from a knowledge perspective. This data can allow us to analyze trends and keep us ahead of our competition by using it wisely to make decisions about planning our next steps and changes. I now challenge you to be the expert on examining that knowledge based on your particular area and your particular goals.

# CHAPTER 4

# Lowering Stress, Increasing Quality of Life, and Finding Balance

Unfortunately, many of my clients experience very high levels of stress. They are often overwhelmed by all the responsibilities that come along with their property. For instance, if they moved from single-family investing and bought a thirty-unit, multi-family building, they'll likely be impacted by many of the new challenges and tasks that need to be completed. This is especially true while you're in the process of expanding your portfolio and now have a variety of property types.

Most often, tasks related to rental properties are time-sensitive. If you bought a brand-new building, it is common that the most immediate thing to be done is to distribute a welcome letter that updates tenants on expectations now that you are the new owner. Landlord helpers can be of great value with this task. My company has welcome letter templates that are ready to distribute at the click of a button. In addition, we also create a set of invoices and an information sheet. All of this goes out in the mail (thanks to you proactively requesting tenant contact info from the prior owner!) so that they have it and there's no a delay in funds. This is key.

Providing these in combination lowers stress and raises productivity for our clients because you now have somebody assisting you who has experience in this line of work, as opposed to the stress involved with training someone on tasks you know. What we then try to do is to talk to the existing landlord about how the service we offer helped realign and set professional expectations for the tenants.

Sometimes what ends up happening to a newer landlord who is trying to grow business is that they seek to accommodate every tenant request without evaluating the consequences of setting expectations that cannot be met throughout the terms of the lease. At times an accommodation made without the proper benefit of the noted exception to policy can cause unnecessary disappointment and conflict at the time of the next request. For example, if the tenant requests new LED bulbs but the policy is not to replace bulbs, the next request may be denied, causing disappointment. Having someone stress the significance of any complimentary adjustments the landlord makes provides a valuable baseline of reference to the lease policies without adding long-term problems. Most real estate investors want to be able to provide top-notch service in a professional, stress-free environment without sacrificing their stability. Your landlord helper will ensure that tenants understand available options that make them feel heard and protected and don't drain your finances. Our role will be to clarify that you offer 24/7 maintenance lines to accommodate various schedules, but make clear that all maintenance requests are not handled at the time of the report, or outside of business hours, unless there is a safety hazard. The ability to report an issue in our 24/7 world is a convenience but does not mandate an immediate resolution. Setting up those communication standards is then viewed as a benefit to the resident and establishes expectations and a reasonable level of convenience. Taking such a step professionalizes the relationship and removes the drama and stress, since human nature drives us to be helpful even when requests may be outside of the lease.

A frequent occurrence of misunderstandings with maintenance requests happens with single-family homes. When someone rents a single-family home, it is very helpful to develop a maintenance cost schedule to be initialed at move in and a copy should be provided for the resident. The maintenance fee schedule will help the resident identify what fees will be involved when calling in issues. This fee schedule provides the resident a clear visual reminder and understanding of what's covered and what's not from a maintenance standpoint. This may be especially helpful if the resident is moving from a multi-family rental apartment where more items were previously repaired without a fee. When we act as the primary point of contact for the resident calls and requests, we can step in to immediately disclose that we will clarify the language on the lease to determine if the incident or item is included. This notification method gives our owners the opportunity to receive the information in a format that makes it conducive to a business decision and affords the opportunity to offer a warm reply with a smaller accommodation. From there, the owner can determine if making an exception will provide a valuable payback in the relationship – without having the stress of dealing with every step leading up to this decision.

A smaller or new landlord also has to focus on deescalating the emotion that goes into the decision, be it from their end or the tenant's. They must depersonalize the situation and not take it as an attack. Simply review the issue and make a rational business decision, considering what's good for you, the property, and your relationship with that tenant.

One of the things new landlords seem to forget is that it is much less expensive to keep an existing tenant than replace one. If this is a relationship you value and the request is of a reasonable nature and not too costly or time-consuming, you may want to go ahead and complete that task, just for the long-term value of tenant satisfaction.

One of the complaints we often hear from new landlords is, "I don't use a real estate agent, or an MLS service because they charge us one month's rent." Let's say, for instance, that rent is $1,200 a month. That equates to $100 in services monthly, for a value that is undoubtedly worth more to your bottom line financially and time-wise.

Why is that? For starters, they may be able to offer that property at $100 higher than you as the small business owner would have. They may attract a stronger clientele. Perhaps the potential tenants have more thorough background information and stronger credit reports as a result of working through a leasing agent. Then, of course, the fee even becomes less if they have them sign a two- or three-year lease. They're still charging you the flat fee of one month's rent. Some leasing agents will charge you one-and-a-half months', rent if they're writing a three-year lease, but that's something you could probably negotiate with them.

In that situation, it didn't cost you anything to utilize a service. In fact, you've gained from it *and* reduced your stress. Beyond the potential of additional monthly income, services will show your property, include the credit checks, and do background checks. They're also generally very comfortable with having you check and read through all tenant information before anything is signed.

One way to further your lower stress is to remove yourself from antagonistic discussions with a tenant. A way to do this is by utilizing a form on a platform such as Google Forms, which is a free way of receiving and tracking maintenance requests. Implementing forms will allow the flexibility to track in a spreadsheet format to be used at year-end for analysis. Sometimes the use of that alone deescalates everybody's emotions because it allows the tenant time to cool down and calmly list what the issue is. The landlord can then professionalize the situation and calmly see that request as something other than an attack on them or their property. Many of your residents would prefer the convenience of an electronic form as a simple and convenient way to report a request.

When your landlord helper serves as your point of contact for maintenance requests, they should also be spending time to understand exactly what the core issue is. For example, someone may call in stating that their air conditioner doesn't work. That, as we know, can mean many things. Is the unit itself not turning on? Do you hear air cycling through? Is it cycling through and not blowing hot air? The key is to get to the point so both time and money are saved when addressing the issue. A good landlord helper will always take this approach.

One of the things that most often comes up when we talk about lowering stress and improving quality of life is that as most landlords will tell you, the hardest thing can be the inability to go on vacation.

Another aspect that we're able to assist with is vacations or time away. You'll inevitably take time out-of-office and we ensure that the ball isn't dropped when you're gone. You may think that this could easily be handled by family or friends, but in most cases, they won't have the proper training to do the job as well as a landlord helper would. This includes emergency repair situations that your friends or family would definitely not be equipped to address. They also may not treat the responsibilities with the same priority you do, and something may fall through the cracks.

When we talk about lowering stress and improving quality of life, we know that everyone's thresholds and needs vary. There's a tendency to think that rent collection and maintenance are the key pain points to being a landlord, but it is really the large variety issues you'll deal with day to day that cause your stress to mount. To minimize and control this, take time to understand the areas of your business that can be streamlined, delegated, or even eliminated. Work is only one aspect of your life. Prioritize efficiency and balance and both you and your business will thrive.

# CHAPTER 5

# Increasing Cash Flow and Balancing Finances

You've acquired a building whose properties you want to rent, so your bottom line is to make money. Websites such as the MLS, Trulia, Craigslist, and Rentometer can give you an idea of what to charge for rent.

Because you've prepared, you have a list of your expenses, your margin, real estate taxes, padding, an idea of how many days vacant a year you might have, and how much money you expect to make. Keep in mind what we have said in previous chapters: there's also a human element to this process. We're not just buying shoes at one price and reselling them at the next. In this particular case, the thing that's going to impact your bottom line more than anything is finding the right tenants and making sure that you've done an adequate job of screening them. You can surely fill the building immediately, but are you filling it with the correct people? And are you filling it for a long-term relationship? As a new landlord, the tenant screening process is an area where you *must* focus your attention.

Many people will tell you to "hire slow and fire fast." The same principal can apply to the rental process. "Hiring slow" means reading through applications in a thorough manner and doing proper screening. This should include more than just a credit and background check. Follow through with calls to previous employers, landlords, and references. We suggest open-ended questions that might enlighten you on behavior that is most closely aligned to your expectations in a new resident.

Take your time in reviewing this a potential residents credit report as well. There's a reason that presenters at real estate conferences do full presentations on how to examine and understand each line. For example, a collection: There's a vast difference between an unpaid medical bill due to an ongoing dispute versus someone not making their car payments. In both situations, we should do our due diligence to understand the full situation, especially in these economic times when people's scores may have suffered due to a market crash or bad investment.

Understand that the right tenant will affect the guarantee of receiving good cash flow monthly. Again, keep in mind the stories of someone asking to put down three months' rent. They may be able to because they didn't pay the last landlord and they were evicted. Something like this may not immediately show up on a credit report. So always proceed with caution, do your research, and don't just get excited by the "green."

Another area to examine on the credit report is how long the potential tenant has lived in their last few homes to establish if they'll be likely to stay for a while or move when the one-year lease ends. If somebody's had the same job for years or the same home, that's a great sign that they may be grounded in routines.

In today's economy, with rents steadily on the rise, people are not moving every year. If they must move, perhaps it's to expand or because of a job in a new part of town. But because rents are increasing, tenants are tending to want to stay with their existing landlord. If the credit history shows lots of movement, be sure to ask about it and listen closely.

To further expand on placing the right tenant, the next thing you're going to look for is what impact the eviction process would have on your dollar. The eviction process can definitely cost you anywhere from one month's rent to the equivalent of six months' rent. When I say the equivalent of, it's because in addition to the lost rent, you would also be paying a lawyer, attorney fees, and court fees. Be familiar with your county and city laws that specifically pertain to tenant and landlord rights. That could really impact your level of effort to get a bad tenant removed from the property.

I once listened to an interview with someone sharing a personal situation. Before he bought a building, he said that he wanted to be sure that his rental cash flow could replace a modest base salary. His cash flow was at $3,500 a month, the rough equivalent to a $36,000 salary. This amount would give him the comfort he needed to leave his current job.

To play it safe, he decided to instead double that number and require $7,000 in cash flow per month. At the end of that first year, he did not end up with any cash flow. Here he had thought he had put together a reasonable plan, but because of unexpected furnace replacements, increases in real estate taxes, different financing costs, and unplanned repairs, he was left with nothing at the end of year one. Real estate investing takes time and proper planning for that time.

As illustrated by the example, when building a potential cash flow, you must take a conservative, very high-risk approach to calculating those numbers and still make sure that the building, the people you're selecting, and the numbers all shake out in order to increase that cash flow. Include buffers for unexpected repairs and even paying off the mortgage early. And be wise to the fact that due to the nature of this business, it is never as simple as assuming all factors are captured in your spreadsheet because humans are involved.

Remember that there are many human factors involved and there are going to be many situations that are outside of your control. How do you avoid that? Find mentors and analyze similar buildings and their attributes so you can plan for any potential change in cost based on historical trends.

Lumber prices, for example, just skyrocketed. If you were looking at lumber prices from two years ago and doing your estimate on a rehab, your numbers wouldn't even be close. Keep in mind, there are certain items that are speculative in cost by nature so when you're putting together your spreadsheet to determine what you can be expected to make, ensure that those numbers are in line when it comes to rehab.

Another consideration is whether the unit is what we refer to as "make ready." That refers to the state of the apartment as it relates to turnaround time needed to rehab for the next tenant. This may not be an area where much thought is generally spent, but there is big money to be won and lost in this process.

When somebody is going to be leaving the unit, the earlier you know that, the better. If you have a good office process that identifies those people proactively and you have a good relationship with the existing tenant, you should be able to begin making repairs before they leave. If there are small items that need to be fixed, maybe doors adjusted, cabinet knobs screwed on tighter etc. this should be happening prior to the current tenant leaving.

There are obviously some tasks, such as carpet cleaning, that you don't want to do again and again. You don't want to double your costs, but you do want to think wisely about beginning what you can and then trying to bring down that vacancy to zero. Interestingly, there were times where people didn't count on zero. They went with thirty days and sixty days, the latter of which would be a foolish number to count on in the current economic times. You should absolutely not be sixty days in between units unless you have major rehab work that you have to go through. And that would signal to me that you're almost gutting and modernizing the unit. Remember, being mindful of cash flow at all times is what keeps your investments steady and growing.

When we talk about increasing cash flow and balancing finances, there are other tips that you can move to as well. Let's take your real estate taxes, for instance. Real estate taxes take a large percent out of most people's expense category. There are real estate attorneys who do nothing but specialize in appealing your taxes. You can find different rates, but generally, they'll charge you for the first year and depending on which county you're in, that's an expense that is usually based on the percent of savings. Let's say the dollar amount savings will last for approximately two to three years and the payment that you've made for getting the savings is only one. You pay once but the impact of that appeal lingers over the next couple years. So, if you follow that cycle again, my savvy investors, you should appeal every single year.

Seek to set up the right relationship in your respective county. In some, that relationship must be with an attorney, who is required by law to specialize in real estate tax. Once you've established a connection and you've found the best person for the job, your time will be efficiently spent.

# CHAPTER 6

# The Evolution of the Property Management World

We now live in a world where communication is at the forefront of everything, thanks to many technological advances. People are very well connected with their cellphones, tablets, and computers. But interestingly, the property management industry has been one of the slower areas to adopt the many new options. Understanding how pivotal technology that helps you work smarter can be, my company launched a new, web-based application back in 2010 to accept automatic payments. This was the game changer we knew it would be. Yet surprisingly, even in 2017, the industry doesn't have full adoption of tools like this across the board.

There are certain communities that are slow to adapt to electronic payments, better known as ACH payments.

### The Automated Clearing House Network

The ACH Network is at the center of commerce in the U.S., moving money and information from one bank account to another through Direct Deposit and Direct Payment via ACH transactions, including ACH credit and debit transactions; recurring and one-time payments; government, consumer and business-to-business transactions; international payments; and payments plus payment-related information. Each year it moves more than $40 trillion and nearly 23 billion electronic financial transactions, and currently supports more than 90 percent of the total value of all electronic payments in the U.S. As such, the ACH Network is now one of the largest, safest, and most reliable payment systems in the world, creating value and enabling innovation for all participants.

ACH Network: Quick Facts

The ACH Network is a batch processing system in which financial institutions accumulate ACH transactions throughout the day for later batch processing. Instead of using paper to carry necessary transaction information, such as with checks, ACH Network transactions are transmitted electronically, allowing for faster processing times and cost savings.[1]

Some communities as slower to adopt ACH merely because they're not necessarily banking communities, but other communities have adapted quickly to using Chase Quick Pay. You can liken this shift to the evolution of cellphones utilizing Google Pay or Apple Pay to purchase coffee, clothing, and more. It will be interesting to watch and adapt to new changes as they impact the rental industry going forward, and then realize the lag in some cases.

The second role that we see technology affecting relates to rent strategy. Yes, there is regular thought that goes into established prices outside of when a tenant vacates. The process and technology involved are very similar to what a day trader does and we see the same type of technology being implemented in large national property management firms. Those firms have eliminated the task of the leasing agent, who traditionally negotiated the rate was on a specific unit. Now software programs assign rates on such units daily through algorithms. The algorithms also look at how quickly units are being leased and how competitors are pricing their apartments. As we know, location and amenities in one building can be specific to units with views, and take into account stairs and elevators when determining the cost on higher floors.

---

[1] What is ACH?: Quick Facts About the Automated Clearing House (ACH) Network. (2015, October 01). Retrieved October 26, 2016, from https://www.nacha.org/news/what-ach-quick-facts-about-automated-clearing-house-ach-network

In other words, you could go in one day and get quoted one price, and the next see a completely different price simply due to availability. It's a cool thing to see the impact of technology in a role like that and how it trickles down. Even though most of the smaller investors are not utilizing these programs we expect to see more advances in this area going forward. Investors at one time could not price units without multiple calls to create a spreadsheet on amenities. Investors have some confidence that when searching online, most of the numbers reflect a good basis for a real-time market value, and can arrive at a solid starting price accordingly. Rentometer and Zillow also provide a lot of valuable statistics on what something has rented for in the area. Keep in mind actual rents received for a lease agreement may not always be factual, as opposed to a home purchase where there is a title company recording the legal amount on the documents.

Landlord helpers also share this type of information with our clients. We do this with landlords to keep them well educated on that process and the value of doing research so that they can be getting the most dollars for their particular units.

Another communication or technology tool that we see being used is from the maintenance perspective. You will find dedicated maintenance apps that help you track maintenance at a web-based level, as opposed to pushing paper. Use have a digital repository of their maintenance requests and history, making it easy to track costs and determine any patterns.

This allows the landlord to enter the details of what needs to be fixed and then dispatch to the phone of the maintenance worker, who of course has the coordinating application, so that they can see the details of the transaction. Before investing in this software, evaluate if it is the most cost-effective for the size of your operation; you should still be studying and gathering best practices from what is offered.

Perhaps instead you might take advantage of a voice text system such as Google Voice, which is free. This service also allows you to send texts from your computer, where a history is kept. What that does is really streamline requests and hold everybody accountable to transmitting accurate information, such as name, phone number, the issue, and whether there a work order number.

You could also attach a picture file to the item for the maintenance worker so they understand visually what needs to happen. He can reciprocate and send images once the work is completed. Again, with a service like Google Voice, all of this would be stored for quick access in the future.

One of the most common issues that all the landlords face is a clogged toilet resulting from items being put in and flushed. Advances in technology allow us to see exactly what is causing the blockage, take images, and then charge the tenant if this was due to their negligence. In the past, this certainly wouldn't have been a quick, in-and-out determination! This is a good, simple illustration of how technology can save us time and money.

Another aspect is for routing service calls. Think about UPS and how efficiently they run. Software exists that you can also apply to your maintenance workers' schedules, maximizing their day through analysis of the most effective routes and more.

I recently heard in a local presentation that Craigslist is still responsible for around 26% of leads, followed closely by Zillow at 23%, 14% from the MLS, 3% being a sign on the building, and 2% being the newspaper. This is just a snapshot in time for one particular month being evaluated, but it does represent a pretty accurate picture of how leads are being generated in our current market.

One of the other things that we discuss with our clients is what generates action on your ad. We see the impact of technology with more and more photos. With the advent of cellphone photography, it's now a simple task for the most amateur landlords to get images and even video. Keep in mind that even as a small landlord, if you have a multi-family unit where many of the units are similar, one professional or even semi-professional video of that particular unit can be reused until you remodel!

Technology plays a huge role in the way we approach marketing to new tenants; we give them the visual of the images and movies. What that allows us to do is have a more accurate caller on the line. Now, most of your residents are doing a lot of pre-screening. There will never be a replacement for actually seeing a unit, but a lot of shopping is done online, especially in the world of real estate. A good picture or video can equal a sale, or loss thereof!

Texting has caused another major shift. It has become such a common form of communication that not embracing it as a landlord could result in a lost lead. Neglecting this process directly ties to your bottom line and the lead process. A lot of thought needs to go into using the latest technologies to making sure you're covering and crossing socio-economic lines. Additionally, people use their cellphone to do their pre-screening, so you must be on top of your technology so you don't miss that call.

How do I not lose that lead? Maybe by having an instant text message or an auto-reply for a certain email address you use. That solution is simple, free, and you don't have to buy sophisticated software. You could use a Gmail address just for that and use an auto-responder, something that immediately alerts that tenant that you have received their interest. The same goes for text messages. More people are texting that speaking on the phone these days. You can text while at work and have something in place to be able to text that person back so you don't lose leads you spent so much time and effort for. The reality is that the landlord world has greatly evolved and you must keep up in order to sustain and build.

While we think of Facebook as a social tool, the reality is it has the numbers behind it. Whether or not you choose to engage in disclosing your personal life on Facebook, the reality is if I have a unit for rent, there are people in that social forum who can get that message out quickly. It's in my best interest to create some kind of Facebook presence to be advertising just as much as the Trulia, Craigslist, and the like. Many of our landlords create a Facebook or Twitter business page to advertise vacancies and promote their community with unit images and updated events.

Whether you are a formal apartment complex owner or you are a small landlord, you want to be sure that you are engaging. Facebook is used by 1.59 billion people, so it would be prudent to utilize its reach. The takeaway is that you *need* technology and *need* to feel comfortable with it, or find resources that are. And while real estate is a people business, to reach those people we have to embrace the technological advancements that can simplify our lives as well as extend our voice.

# CHAPTER 7

# Customization and Communication

The value of communication is immeasurable, specifically as it pertains to the residents in your building. In the previous chapter, we talked about the impact of technology on our communication skills with our residents and how a landlord needs to spend time honing in on this. Being in the instant world we are in, we know that whether it comes to ordering your Christmas presents or ordering a birthday present, we now all have the ability and strong expectation that we'll have it a day or two later.

The same applies to the expectation that your tenants have. They want and expect that same type of instant gratification. Many larger communities utilize online resident portals as a quick way for residents to be able to communicate amongst each other and with management. They simply log on, select their task, complete, and submit. Smaller business owners can also take advantage of these efficiencies through automation. Perhaps you may consider a website with forms available for tenants to submit to an email address, a distribution list to quickly reach your tenants, or creating a community on Facebook to allow them to communicate with each other.

Depending on the size of your portfolio, you may be at the stage where you are considering various property management web-based solutions. As you scale your business, you may need to consider a landlord helper as a solution to dive deep into technology-based solutions without negatively impacting your schedule. If you have not already implemented a web-based property management solution, you should at a minimum consider expanding by implementing Google Forms to collect information from your tenants. From application information and maintenance requests to move-out and forwarding address forms, the ability to collect data is a fundamental tool needed in your management toolbox.

The desire for an instant answer also makes it difficult for landlords to say that calls 24/7 are not acceptable. Remember, a tenant isn't necessarily demanding an answer at night, but they have to be able to log their request somewhere in real time so that they at least know it's recorded based on their schedule. When my company works with specific landlords to customize a plan, this is a consideration.

Another key insight I would like to share with you concerns the value of communication and training. If you are a new landlord, or perhaps growing into large multi-family communities, you might look to lenders for property management training. On multiple occasions, I have trained multi-family landlords for a not-for-profit lender in the Chicago area that provides property management training for real estate investors. The investors come with a wide variety of experiences; they were either first-time landlords or those who jumped in but were now seeking the advantage of good management training skills. Sometimes it was be the investor's first venture into scaling into the sizeable task of buying a larger multi-family investment, and so this type of property management training brought together several experts from various fields to contribute to the basic knowledge that they see brings success for other investors as they begin managing their buildings. We had tax appeal experts there to speak who helped address the need to lower costs to produce more income on the property. My job was to speak to technology and how landlords can use that to professionalize their relationships with tenants. There were other people there who would speak specifically about marketing and how landlords could best market their buildings.

Another aspect of communication is educating yourself on what to expect from the tenants about their rights while occupying your property. A landlord should be very familiar with the Residential Landlord and Tenant (RLT) Ordinance. This document outlines the laws and expectations of the city as it pertains to the lease. If a landlord violates this agreement, they are subject to fines. The John Marshall Fair Housing Legal Support Center and Clinic provides legal assistance in the City of Chicago to educate tenants on housing laws. In many cases, legal representation is free to the tenant.

If they can find an error in that lease, or learn of the landlord making an error during the eviction process such as a wrong unit number appearing on the legal notice, they can use that to have their case dismissed from court. Again, that bears repeating. The case can get dismissed because of that *one* error. Now, what really must be understood is that the free attorney that I mentioned for tenants is not always free to you. When a landlord loses the case, they will be paying the free attorney's legal fees, because if you've ever looked at a lease carefully, it says that whoever wins will pay the other's legal fees. This is on top of any lost rent.

While the service is free for the tenant, if their services provide the value of winning the case then the attorneys do get paid, but by the landlord's loss of whatever the judge deemed. You can see it would be very advantageous for the law firm to try to find that error, because while they offer free services, they ultimately do get paid if they win that case. That's a crucial piece of information when it comes to a new landlord class.

Consider exploring your legal system so you know whether you have the right documents. And are you filling them out correctly? So many times, we see new landlords decide that they don't want to pay a lawyer, and understandably so; there's not a lot of profit on buying rental properties when you start. But you want the best lease you can to start with, including clauses. Contact an attorney or attend an REIA group in your area to research the legal forms and laws specific to your county and the proper format. A new landlord or one expanding their portfolio should not cut corners on consulting an attorney. Scaling up without having a good lease may be a very costly mistake down the line. You can search for help on free housing clinics in your area, or contact the Realtors Association for guidance on good real estate investment attorneys if you do not have a local REIA group.

Know what resources are available to your tenant. For example, imagine if your current tenant would not allow you to show the unit prior to them vacating. If they would not allow you to show while they're still in it, then that means if they leave on August 31st, there will be nobody there September 1st unless you can sell it strictly with pictures on the Internet. Most families, obviously, want to view a new residence first hand so you have reduced your odds of a quick money-saving turnover.

At best, you might be starting a lease on September 15th and at worst November 1st. In certain areas of the country, the renting season is over past October 1st, so you may not have a tenant until the new year. This illustrates one of the many reasons why advice from a lawyer and receiving clauses for your leases is pivotal. With the proper verbiage, if your tenant resists allowing you to show the unit, it would be clear that they could be penalized.

When seeking an attorney, look for one that specifically works a lot with rental cases. Ask around and get referrals. You want to work with someone who has been through the full gamut of potential issues.

Circling back to customization, this comes up because of different demographics and needs. Because of the school system, for example, we see that more and more of the states are offering earlier and earlier start dates to school. As more schools are opening pre-Labor Day as opposed to post-Labor Day we're seeing that the last big day for move-ins is starting to trend closer to August 1st, where at one time the largest moving day of the year was always September 1st.

That *was* a national statistic. What does that mean to you? It means that you may want to look for your leases to expire between April 30th and at the latest, July 31st. If you do have a brand-new resident starting a lease on a less popular month (i.e. October 1st or November 1st), you'll want to consider either an 18-month lease that takes them into the following spring, or an early lease, and suggest an early termination of May 31st. It's all in how you present it, because it's not just to your advantage as a landlord, it's to the tenant's advantage as well. When that lease does expire, it gives the resident the most options and the largest variety of homes to select from. It puts the landlord at a better season for attracting more residents. This is important to the landlord so he or she does not make the mistake of settling for an application background where they may feel some doubts. Many of our clients' biggest regrets come from large amounts of money lost because they accepted a resident knowing the upfront risk factors and ignoring all the signs in desperation to sign a lease.

As a landlord helper, we provide our clients the ability to customize a plan that addresses their specific wants and needs. We listen carefully to our landlords, dissecting their roadblocks and determining where in the system they need to add process. We also tackle aspirations they have for their portfolio, which enables my company develop a winning customized plan that we can help them implement. Most clients come to us when they are planning for growth in their real estate portfolio. They are seeing missed opportunities to purchase and recognize that in order to experience phenomenal growth, they need assistance keeping up with daily tasks. They want and need to implement safeguards to their process to prevent tasks from slipping, possibly resulting in small losses that can quickly snowball into critical funding gaps. They prefer to eagerly practice their expertise in acquisitions. Sometimes large portfolio investors find that using a service to supplement peak periods that overwhelm their internal staff provides the focus they need on superior customer service and reduced collection losses.

# CHAPTER 8

# Embracing Technology to Sell More Products

Technology is having a major impact on the property management process, just as it is in every other industry. In many cases, complicated and detailed new technologies are required to be a game changer. Disruptive, new, and impactful technologies do not have to be the result of years of engineering research.

Take Uber, for example. While it still simply provides an automobile to pick you up, the company has added a few conveniences via some simplified changes to their computer application, and in turn, has completely changed the taxi industry. Really, there's nothing at all new about the process; Uber has just added convenience. They've simply put a golden touch on it with technology to make it easier and more personal.

Thinking back to Chapter Six, where we touched on some of the changes that we've seen in payments, I would say we really haven't seen what I'll call the "disruptive" technology yet in the rental sector. But we've certainly seen the importance of simplifying processes and increasing convenience, just as Uber did with the taxicabs and shared rides.

We see that the same has been true in the marketing world, where technology is really shifting from standard ads to a heavy concentration on social media.

Platforms like Facebook and Snapchat provide opportunity for specific and far reach to customers.

We're going to be seeing more and more people doing something as simple as going on their Facebook or other social media and posting Live videos while on a property as a new form of open house. It is so interesting, and definitely different from the days of simply posting only pictures on a listing. Soon investors like realtors will be implementing virtual makeover images to enhance the buyer's imagination when viewing rooms that may need décor updating.

Another improvement possibility is with drones. Drones show the overview of a whole area, which can help someone pick a specific location. It is hard to fully grasp how your home may back up to a wetland, a nature trail, etc. in still photos. A drone, however, can capture it all thanks to its aerial and 360-degree abilities. Including a component like this to your listing takes it to the next level and allows your potential customer the ability to not have to imagine key aspects of the property; they're seeing it from all angles!

What we're already seeing at some of the higher-level properties are virtual reality tours, which require glasses to be worn and provide the viewer with an experience that makes them feel as if they're inside. While currently utilized only with very high-end homes, as with all other technology, before you know it the innovation will be commonplace for all listings.

Many of these things can be intimidating to some landlords. But if you are keeping up with the likes of Bigger Pockets, seminars, webinars, and attending REIA meetings, you will be abreast of all the latest offerings. To be successful, it's going to be more and more important to stay in a connected community.

Another specific area that will be important for smaller landlords to keep up with are smart houses. These may include thermostats that are controlled through a computer, fingerprint deadbolt locks, and more. It is imperative to keep up with such improvements, at least to an extent, in order to compete with the offerings of many brand-new buildings constantly being built. Implementing next-generation technologies into your properties will also offer significant appeal to someone considering moving in, or on the reverse, moving out. You'll appear to be offering the convenience of the big associations or neighborhood residential properties, but instead offering the privacy of the smaller, most intimate setting.

A landlord can achieve this is through improved and streamlined communication. Earlier we talked a little bit about technology tools that can keep you communicating, and this is key because that's going to give your tenant the sense of a personal touch.

One example, for instance, is our newsletter. We talk with our clients often about having an electronic newsletter that would go to each resident each month. To expand on that, we make sure that such a newsletter includes video. Again, it is something as simple as taking a smartphone and doing some clever videoing of stores in the area or what's happening in your area.

Not only is that impactful from the marketing standpoint, but it's also very appealing as a monthly newsletter if you keep it short (we always recommend 60 seconds or less). That's just one way that you can bring your marketing up to par with the latest in technology.

## VIRTUAL REALITY

The industry's next big implementation of virtual reality is to provide it for you as a tool for planning your next vacation. Similar to a virtual open house, you'll be able to see the entirety of the rental you're interested in. Wow!

One of the many great things about technology is that the cost of new technology is less as time goes by. So, before you know it, you'll be able to advertise your home in the same way.

Experts talk about the fact that a real communication platform exists with this virtual reality because of its widespread applicability in so many facets of life. Face-to-face consultations will drastically change. You'll now have the opportunity to do your applicant screening process through a virtual reality tool. We're going to see developers and partners across industries begin to look for this kind of immersive and augmented reality too. Before we know it, this technology will be part of our daily lives.

Architect's jobs will also change significantly, too. Before virtual reality, designing a building and seeking to understand the effectiveness of the many components wasn't as tangible. But with this new development, we'll see that time to market will be reduced as architects will be able to truly visualize the building as a whole. On the reverse, the client/building owner will be able to quickly understand what it really feels like to walk through that building. If an architect thinks this 90-degree turn or this bending wall is "cool," you will get to experience it before it is built!

Years ago, I used to teach software training. An entire floor of a nationwide corporation would be taken over for teaching and demonstrations. While this was a great solution when the ability to experience various situations was needed, with virtual reality now available, this training method is no longer the most effective approach.

With virtual reality, you'll be able to get more and faster feedback. There will still be changes, but with the ability to have more eyes experience it earlier on, you're much more likely to get to market faster with a more solid and well-received product. These are just a few examples that illustrate the exciting advancements we can look forward to within our industry.

I was recently reading Kevin Kelly's book *12 Technological Forces*, in which he talks about increasing efficiency that we feel real-time. If you think about, let's say, an ATM, it's hard to believe that at one time you had to wait in a line inside of a location. Now if you want money, you're able to withdraw at any time, any day of the week. This encourages people to utilize ATMs because they have the control and power. With technological advances in real estate, we seek to do the same thing: empower investors in ways that serve both them and their clients.

Years back when I was delivering technology solutions on databases, it was very hard to take the user who was just sitting at their desktop and have them understand what used to be unobtainable. They had to submit things and they had to be approved, and you gave them a tool right on their desktop so they could analyze the data themselves. This is the same impact we're seeing in the rental market; once these tools start to trickle down, you will have that same level of knowledge.

# BEHAVIOR ANALYSIS

One of the major areas of improvement will be with tracking behavior. If you have shopped on Amazon.com and purchased a pair of cowboy boots, you'll soon realize that the next time you log in you'll receive suggestions to shop for more cowboy boots. It's almost as though they assume you're a boot addict simply based on one purchase. The reality of the situation, however, is that Amazon.com can recall your shopping behavior so that it can make suggestions to you on items that will be appealing based on past purchases.

You have the same experience on Facebook. If you visit a particular website, it is very likely that at some point during your next Facebook visit you'll see an advertisement for that site and other related ones. If you follow specific friends, you'll get more pictures and notices from those friends.

Well, the same technology that's working to sell you in that way will trickle down to the smaller landlord. By investing in social media ads, you'll absolutely receive more interest in that two-bedroom, one-bath home that you're renting. This would be a prime example of you working smarter and not harder while reaping the benefits of the technology available to you.

From a marketing perspective opening up behavior tracking enables you to increase your leads through funnels of targeted consumers. And luckily, these are the least expensive options to reach a large audience. We cannot predict how the landscape will change in the future, but these are all disruptive technologies that are absolutely simplifying everyday life. And as evolution is continual, we can expect that the advances will just get better and better.

# APPLICATION PROCESS

As we know it, the application process is primarily paper-based. Yes, we currently have a tool like DocuSign that allows us to use the email system to send a document for somebody to sign and send it back in an instant, as opposed to waiting days. But as a successful and organized landlord, you need to think ahead. Utilizing technology to advance the screening process will be crucial.

People are digesting information audibly and through all their senses. And this enhanced application process allows for implementation and usage of video, which also engages the aural aspect. This is important because people are using their auditory senses to gain further information. For instance, we use the analogy of Audible, which is one of the many current audiobook providers that exist. It is incredible to think of the lifecycle of books, beginning in paper format, then Kindle, and now as audiobooks. You should want the same type of advancement for your properties; a hosting platform that contains all of your properties, the application, and an upload functionality for video submission is the perfect way to accomplish this.

We see that even in the hiring process, companies requiring applicants to provide a multimedia component as part of their application submission, versus the traditional, flat paper resume. There'll be places for all the various ways of digesting information as we move forward through the rental process, through the residents, through the landlords, and through those options. And that's just one way of managing all that information.

As has been detailed, there are many technological advancements which can be used to improve move-out communications and inspections, and small investors can reap major benefits from these too. So, keep an eye on ways to implement all these technologies in order to continue looking toward the future and keeping up with the trends. And again, if this isn't your forte, seek help from a savvy assistant!

The whole idea of immersing yourself in these options to implement total *look, hear, see*, and *feel* communications with your tenants is very important. And these efforts will mean a lot when it comes to the property management of your building, in addition to refining and streamlining your communication style.

## MOBILE TECHNOLOGY

We cannot speak about technology without acknowledging the advances in texting. Mobile technology is so much more in people's lives that they are going to want to do things on the move. So what can you implement that is going to give them that kind of 365-day feel? What are those technologies that will make them feel surrounded, and from a management standpoint, give you the most comprehensive and functional reports? What technologies will help you be more receptive to tenants because you'll be implementing systems that tell you first that, for example, the heat is not working correctly, prior to them even calling you?

Additionally, all these technological advances are going to help you attract and retain the right tenants. You don't have to implement the most expensive things, because we see these costs to entries going smaller and smaller. But customer service is key. It's going to be more and more key, and in order to keep the best tenants, you're going to want to be able to be on track with it. Make sure you're looking out to the horizon for these changes. It's going to be a central part of your job to keep up with that.

Take texting, for example. Texting has evolved significantly from its origins of alphanumeric character limitations. Next will come video texting, where a landlord can send information to the client, or vice versa. Again, it is another huge step forward in being thorough and providing a full picture of the topic at hand.

A greater mobile presence also allows for a 24-hour help desk. There has been a surge in content added to YouTube regarding home repairs. Creating 60-second video on how to change a filter, on where the release is for the garbage disposal, or on how to turn off the water to the home if there were to be a bad leak in cold temperatures, can result in very helpful links in a portal or email blasts to send to tenants and will, in turn, save you the time of addressing many individual questions. Tenants will have the information at their fingertips to be accessed at any hour, so if you are unable to answer your phone, they have the information that they need.

# CHAPTER 9

# Money-saving Tips for Real Estate Investing

When you're first considering putting some big chips on the table to get involved with your first property, it is normal to experience a little bit of fear. In order the alleviate some of that, these are some things that you want to consider.

## THE SPREAD

I recently heard a good example of somebody with their very first property in the Dallas-Forth Worth area. This owner talked about being able to obtain a $60,000 property that they'd be able to rent for $1100 per month. Let's examine those numbers.

You're going to pay $60,000 for the property and invest another $10,000 in improvements. Let's assume you're mortgaging or getting some kind of a loan. For the sake of our example, a $65,000 loan at 3.92% (a current going rate), would equate to monthly payments of $307. Keep in mind, that doesn't include many other expenses like your insurance and real estate taxes, but it gives you a baseline number to anticipate cash flow. For a moment, put appreciation to the side and consider that just a bonus.

Different people have different rules or formulas as to how much that cash flow should be, but the point is, that's the number you focus on first. Whatever your level of comfort is on what kind of spread you're looking for, remember that's not a solid spread. It can get absorbed by fixed expenses like real estate taxes, so that's got to get added in.

In this example, I'm only using the mortgage payment to give you a brief idea of what to look at. It would be great if the bottom line was that you'd subtract the mortgage of $307 from $1100 and net a cool $793 a month. However, there are other considerations. In reality, you'd be considering a mortgage payment, insurance, and your real estate taxes. You might consider also adding in a number for a month this might be vacant per year. You also want to take into consideration any repair costs.

For this example, after all costs are accounted for, your profit may be reduced to $500 a month or as little as $300. The point is that you're looking for that spread and you need to be certain what that is.

## PARTNERSHIP

If you're looking for your first deal, another thing you might want to consider is adding a partner to the equation. If, for instance, you're unable to afford the required down payment, an experienced partner with a like mindset can be more than willing to provide half of that down payment. This is especially true if they are someone who has worked with real estate and they know the benefits of investing.

Because this is your first investment, more than likely you'll be the one who is doing all the work because they are the ones who are essentially allowing you to even get into the deal by giving you that other half.

A lot of people are concerned about partners, and rightfully so. Whether it's in business, life, or marriage, partners are a complicated thing, and there's certainly a give and take. But I would say that partners can be a good option if you are comfortable with them and comfortable knowing that you're both agreeing on the risks involved in real estate. To ensure things don't get too advanced for this first go-round, it is smart to begin with a less expensive property. You want to keep your risk exposure as minimal as possible.

The great thing is that next to most of the nicest neighborhoods, there's an area close by that might have something a little bit more affordable. This is what we refer to as a B or C class property, such as a small single-family home. The idea is to make sure this is an event that is comfortable for you and that the amount of risk that you're taking is reduced.

## B, C, AND WORKING PROPERTIES

One of the other investment strategies can involve buying working-class homes. They might still be B level, but they might be at a little higher level or in a little better area. What that slightly better area will do is bring up the level of tenants who want to live in your area and bring to it a more responsible level of tenants. This could be in areas where schools and things will tie tenants more to the community and will increase their ability to pay and their capacity to want to stay in the unit.

So, the capacity to pay in addition to the ability to want to stay in that area and have stronger job background makes that a little bit easier than somebody going into a major city. Take Chicago, for instance. We have people who will invest specifically in our C properties in challenging areas because there are really low prices, so it represents a low point of entry for a brand-new investor. However, they must be prepared for the challenges that will go with that area.

Challenges in some of those areas can be as simple as loitering, which can sometimes lead to other things. You must be exposed enough to know your market and realize the additional challenges that may go with it. We work with lots of successful investors who choose specifically those areas because they can get into more buildings, but realize that going into C-levels does bring additional challenges. But if there is interest, how to work around the challenges can be learned. Look for experienced investors in those areas who can give you good tips on how to prevent that type of issue. We have very good tenants in those areas. The very good tenants will help also by communicating information to you.

A lot of investors will tell you that if you're going into those more challenging areas, there are tips on how to develop a bond or relationship with some of the tenants in the building. Doing so can help fill that building with solid people because solid people are always looking for peace of mind.

Something as simple as having a building with a well-lit exterior can prohibit loitering and illegal activities from happening. Finding the property and then changing the atmosphere of that property to be sure that it's welcoming, clean, well-lit, and signals to people that there's someone there watching that property can lead to a great start for you and happy tenants.

## THE COST OF BORROWED MONEY

One of the factors that should always weigh into your decision is understanding the cost of the money that you'll need to borrow on that property. I gave the example just above of a 3.92% interest rate. Depending on how many other properties you have, it's important to know that as an investor, you'll only be able to get a limited number of investment properties at a more reasonable rate. Once you start to own more property, you'll move into a different rate quote from the banks and lenders because at that point, lenders will not be able to loan you money because it's now specifically for investment property, in which case different rates go into effect. Those rates are generally higher.

You can also get what people refer to as private money. For instance, over these last few years, it's been easier than ever to get private money because somebody with a lot of wealth and a lot of accumulated money cannot get a good return on their money at the bank, so they're more than willing to loan to you, the investor. This is especially true of those who are familiar with real estate as an investment vehicle for their money. They will allow you to take the money and use it for a down payment or even to carry the mortgage with the loan privately because they know they can ask you, for instance, for five to eight percent. They can't get anywhere near that at a bank.

Now, if you're dealing with a hard-money lender, those rates might be significantly higher because sometimes a hard-money lender will evaluate the level of experience you have. If you are new to the investing world, you're not going to get the same rate as somebody who has already turned over 20 properties.

One of the REIA meetings I recently attended had a panel of three different lenders on the panel. At that panel, they discussed what expectations they have of real estate investors when they request money. One of the things they mentioned was putting together a portfolio of all the properties that you have purchased, or in this case, if it's your very first one, putting together a portfolio of all the ones you looked at and showing them that you have the wherewithal and knowledge to investigate the areas and investigate them thoroughly.

You can find many of these sample spreadsheets and templates on sites like Biggerpockets.com. Utilize these to put your best foot forward and be well educated. You're not going into the scenario not knowing, for instance, what three other houses were on the block. There are so many things in public records. You can show what those houses sold for, maybe what their appraised value is currently, and what type of work was put into those properties. Some of those numbers will have to be speculative if you don't know the owners. Nonetheless, if you're trying to get your very first loan this way, you have to put something together in the form of what you'll refer to as your portfolio, even if it just means a small book of statistics or spreadsheets, which may include what the rate is for employment in the area, or what the job outlook is in the area.

Putting together all those types of reports, while it may seem like an intense amount of paperwork and research, says a lot to the lender and absolutely puts you above somebody else when you're in that first-time investor position.

If you already have properties, gather the relevant information into a portfolio for your potential lenders. What did you spend on your properties? What have you invested in? What are your current incoming rental rates? What does your rental income look like? Answering these questions makes clear to them that they're not dealing with somebody who is not well organized or is just expecting them to approve a loan strictly on the merits of the building (a common fallacy). They're approving a loan not only based on the building, but on your character, your capabilities, and your knowledge of real estate investment in the area.

With the ability to save all of these things in Google Drive or Dropbox, you can be gather all these type of documents and slowly build your portfolio of successful buildings; this makes it much less daunting. Even if you show them mistakes you've made, as long as you have a recap of what the mistakes were, you can easily share these through your Internet document hub. If you are looking to acquire property, let's say once every six months, these are documents that you should have ready.

Since you know you're always on the lookout for the next good deal, these types of documents should be readily available to you in a shared folder that can easily be shared with a specific lender. All you should be doing is updating, for instance, last year's tax return, your last payroll statements, and your last bank statements. But on the whole, the majority of documentation should already be there. Building a portfolio and a history is a very important part of this process when it comes to getting money.

We discussed that there is hard money, private money, and your standard lender. There are all different options for you to get that money. There are many different ways to put together a loan note between you another investor if you used private money or a partner. You want to look into those first, and of course, nothing should get finalized without a comprehensive legal review.

## INCOME AND EXPENSES

Equally important when considering your property is income, and conversely, expenses. You don't want to jump in with the knowledge that expenses are not part of the equation. Sometimes when we don't prepare accurately, we may omit a factor such escalation of property taxes, which usually increase annually.

Depending on the areas you're buying in, the taxes could be $3600 a year, equaling the $300 mortgage payment. That's not something that's going to stay static, however. You'll want to make sure that you're looking ahead over the next five years and assuming an increase. Of course, if you're going to keep the property 30 years, you'll be paying down the loan as well. But if you're planning to ultimately find another property, sell this one and move up, you still want to project that utilities, real estate taxes, and maintenance will likely go up.

Your homeowner's insurance may also be higher than expected, especially when it's used as a rental property, so you'll want to go in knowing that number as an expense and making sure you're shopping around to find the best option. If you talk specifically to an insurance representative that deals with real estate investing, confirm with a reputable person to advise on the deal and determine which options are worth paying for and which may introduce risk if they are not purchased.

For instance, there's specific insurance involved with having the home vacant. If you know that there will be times when the home is going to be vacant, you need to ensure that you're looking at policies that consider that clause, or you want to make sure you're at least aware of it.

It's obviously your personal decision as to what type of insurance is best. There are specific ones in your area, though, so get educated about threats such as thunderstorms, tornadoes, and earthquakes. This is especially true for homes with basements, so you'll want to find out what the options are for things like sump pumps and natural water disasters.

If you bought a multi-family unit, you may or may not need to add in an expense for pest control; some counties require periodic treatments. You may be able to use one of your own maintenance men or a do-it-yourself formula that is now available. If it's a single-family home and your first-time investment, you can mitigate many of the maintenance costs through resident surcharges in the lease.

You'll also always want to remember that while you can push some of those expenses down to the resident, for instance on maintenance and repairs, care of the actual investment property is your responsibility. So, you want to know your tenant's capabilities and know if they're going to make decisions that are good of your investment before you leave all maintenance costs to trickle down to them. They may not always make the repairs in the way you want. You may just add a specific dollar amount that has to be paid on certain repair items. Those are just different ways of structuring a lease to reduce some of the expenses involved with repairs.

Something else to consider is landscaping. If it's a multi-family building, it will be on you to take a look at landscaping budgets. This includes hiring contractors, and of course, you'll want to seek people with experience with multi-family buildings. If you're in an area with snow, the landscaping will usually include pricing for the summer and then the winter with snow removal. You should also consider: Where will your building be on their snow removal route? Are you going to say that they should come out after two inches? How soon do you want them out? You can structure these into your agreement.

When it comes to landscaping, you'll also want to think about whether there are pets in the building and what your expectations are for those tenants when it comes to the landscaping. I have seen specific cases with little buildings – what we refer to three-unit or three-flat buildings – where landscapers have refused to do the landscaping because pet droppings weren't cleaned up. Those are little things, but things you'll want to consider ahead of time when you're putting together this list of expenses and when you work out expectations with your provider as part of those agreements.

Another major consideration when it comes to finances is bookkeeping. Often, a new investor has a line item allowed for legal expenses and accounting each year, but that accounting cost can be controlled by how much or how little bookkeeping work you might do ahead of time and to coding expenses into the right category throughout the year. That's something that you may want to bring somebody in to do once a month just to help prevent the larger costs involved in giving everything to an accountant without preparation.

When we're looking for a new home, we're talking about knowing the area, the property, and whether you can find a smaller first-time investment or should find a partner. Should you buy in an area that's a little more challenging because the prices are extremely low, or should you buy in an area where's there's more job growth? You may also want to be close to a hospital for a more of a semi-professional working neighborhood. A factor like this, as discussed earlier, can potentially mean fewer concerns when it comes to rent being received. Then we want to know the cost of the money involved and add that into the equation.

A couple of other things that need to be looked for in buildings is to consider areas with lower property taxes, as in working neighborhoods, which can vary dramatically. Much of this has to do with the school districts within each area. This is not the case in all states, but it is in many. In areas with lower crime rates, we'll sometimes see higher property taxes. It just really depends on the current state of that government or municipality. The effects all trickle down. Conversely, areas with a growing job market come with many amenities. You'll see the parks, restaurants, and nearby malls, so you'll be able to judge the character.

I've worked with people who do out-of-state investing, which is becoming increasingly popular. In fact, recently I did an interview with somebody out in California regarding international investors. There are even people coming in to buy for-sale land in the U.S. This has become a safe haven for investments because they see good returns.

There are "hot" areas of the country that are considered better investments, especially for out-of-state and international investments. For instance, currently Indianapolis is a very attractive market. Dallas-Fort Worth is also still popular, although the prices have increased so dramatically that it's starting to eliminate some of the investors. Memphis is a very attractive market, as are areas in Kentucky, Tennessee, and of course, Atlanta. The point is to know those markets if out-of-state property might be in the equation for you.

For an effort such as out-of-state investing, you absolutely need to focus on the people element of the relationships involved in your investing. Sometimes for a first-time investor, that might be a little bit more concern than you need to add to the plate. However, if you're in a partnership and you know your partner well, you might feel a little more secure taking on that risk. It's something to think about if out-of-state investing is something that interests you.

In other scenarios, people are just entering the market for investing. They may look for what they refer to as a two-unit or a three-unit apartment building where you can stay in one of those units and still have an investment property. This allows you to take advantage of the lowest mortgage rates because it's considered an owner-occupied dwelling as long as you're in one of those units, and it also allows specific tax benefits when selling it. A long-term investor is usually not looking to sell in a situation similar to what was just described. Rather, they want to hold onto it for a couple of years or whatever the current IRS stipulation is to be qualified for a tax break.

Timelines in such situations affect mortgages as well. Lenders have specific guidelines that they're following to meet those codes so that you can qualify for the best rate, and they will tell you how long you have to live there to be able to get that good rate. You can go ahead and keep that as your first rental assuming you can get cash to flow correctly from the formulas we talked about above. In that case, you should be able to move out of that property, hold onto it for a time, and then move on to your next property.

I know that real estate investments provide you with considerable ability to leverage cash flow, but I highly advise working through your accountant to develop the numbers that are right for you. A related industry term that's very common is the "1031 exchange." This is related to your personal income tax and your ability to defer capital gains on the selling of a property as long as you're rolling it into another property. Generally, there are some strong guidelines governing that, but this situation is ideal for people who are moving up their investment strategy.

If you do implement this strategy, you will want to be sure that you're working with tax advisors who are very well informed on this rule. Those who are in that position can give you a lot of tips and ways to save money. You'll definitely spend money to get that advice, but people who are extremely familiar with the ins and outs on this are extremely valuable to you as the investor. Even if you feel you've studied it, they will have been there and done that, and they will be able to give you specifics that you can work with, commonly referred as the tax loopholes.

Real estate is certainly a "business," but sometimes I think that's too broad a term. People advise you to operate your real estate investing like a business. As we now know though, there are differently sized businesses and everybody has their own best practices. One thing all business owners should do is learn the fundamentals of income vs. expenses and make projections. How do I increase my business? How do I increase my profits?

The same can be said when you are looking at becoming a real estate investor. Have a plan and talk to your tax advisor on the different deductions that are possible. We're talking about a lot of time spent traveling in a car and on the phone, so it is not uncommon to see real estate investors using some type of tablet out in the field for comps and repairs.

Many investors also look to financial advisors and accountants for advice on how to pay their own families to defer some of the profit. This allows you a couple things: You get the opportunity to have your children learn the value of your business and to earn money for the tasks that they can perform, and you're able to write off some of those expenses.

You'll want to work with a very good tax advisor on that to help you structure it so it's all legal and not just a matter of giving your child $20 to go do something. There's a regular, formal process, and it should be handled like the business that it is.

The bottom line for this chapter is that you need to be prepared. In many of the other chapters we refer to the fact that there are resources out there; there is knowledge. There are definitely social media sites that give you the advantage of not making common mistakes.

While being prepared with resources and knowledge can be pivotal, it is important to understand that it will not help you fully avoid mistakes. Your goal in this isn't to be perfect. It's to grow your portfolio and minimize the learning curve to success. So prepare yourself and enjoy the ride. There will be bumps, but preparation can minimize those.

# CHAPTER 10

# Business Organizational skills

Without a doubt, your ability to communicate and use technology plays significant roles in your quest to master success in your real estate investment portfolio. Whether you buy and hold or flip, strong organizational skills will ensure your success in capturing the largest benefits from your investment. A simple guideline to follow is the Triple Constraints of Projects: Quality, Cost, and Schedule.

## THE TRIPLE CONSTRAINT

According to Enterprise PM, a useful online project management source, the triple constraint concept ensures quality. The challenge of every project is to make it work and be successful within the Triple Constraint of quality (scope), cost (resources), and schedule (time). These three elements of a project are known to work in tandem with one another. Where one of these elements is restricted or extended, the other two elements will then also need to be either extended/increased in some way or restricted/reduced in some way. There is a balancing of the three elements that only when fully understood by the Project Manager, allows for the successful planning, resourcing, and execution of a project. At the end of the day, these are the key elements of that will determine whether you have successfully managed a project.[2]

---

[2]    The Triple Constraints of Projects: Quality, Cost and Schedule. Retrieved October 26, 2016, from http://www.enterprise-pm.com/pmbasics/triple-constraint

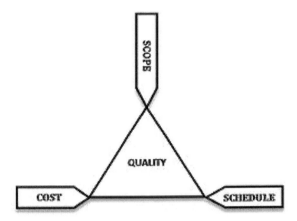

So many pieces of the real estate investment game are based on hard deadlines. From the auction day to the lease expiration and many in between you will want to master the art of staying organized. You may break that down to planning, scheduling, and coordinating but it's important to realize that you have a limited scope of time and resources, so identifying where to seek help becomes an essential part of this skill set.

When you learn the theories behind project management, you review the ultimate relationships of the iron triangle. According to LendingAgile.com:

> *If you change one of the three variables, the physics of project management says that one of the others has to change too. If I want to add scope, time or cost has to go up as well. If I want to deliver in less time, you either need more budget or you need to reduce scope. If you want a less expensive finished product, you either need to reduce scope or reduce the time it takes to build it.* [3]

So how do I work best within these constraints? The ability to master your organizational skills will propel you with a slight edge; the compound effect when it comes time to evaluate delivering is the best-finished product with the most profit.

If you begin to work at breaking up each task of rehabbing a home, filling vacancies or managing the building, we can all think of an investor we know

---

[3]  Cottmeyer, M. (2010, January 28). Replacing the Iron Triangle of Project Management? Retrieved October 26, 2016, from http://www.leadingagile.com/2010/01/replacing-the-iron-triangle-of-project-management/

who is caught up in the details. Who hasn't heard a landlord at a meeting say, "I could hire a lawn service, but I like to cut grass because it is relaxing." While this very well might be true, the bigger truth is if you are trying to grow your portfolio, then identifying the next organizational skill set you need to master would be the better use of your time by far. But like any science, you may fail when you become too adept at mastering each step defined in the detailed analysis. You must focus your strengths on identifying how you can best master delivering the overall plan.

Scheduling is the ability to identify peak periods and staff your resources, or delay your tasks accordingly. The seven days surrounding the first of the month are a peak drain on your resources. The reality of the calendar and clock associated with your lease agreements provides an escalation of tasks and you need to be able to prioritize and delegate them to be both productive and effective in your role. If you plan ahead, you can find tasks that can be anticipated to make you ready.

For example, we suggest identifying residents who will be moving out at lease expiration 60-80 days prior to lease expiration. This gives you ample time to schedule maintenance tasks, key changing, and move out inspection, and to gather information to document the issue of security deposit return. A well-organized landlord with peak organizational skills or a landlord using outside resources will have advertised for new tenants long before lease expiration and ideally will have a new tenant moving in immediately after its expiration.

CHAPTER 11

# Identifying Successful Mentors

In my experience, developing a relationship with someone who has "been there, done that" is invaluable. Each deal in real estate investing will certainly be unique and for the most part, you have already read and heard many stories in your quest for information. You are anxious to move forward.

There are many sources of mentorship and your first steps might include books, podcasts, workshops, and REIA meetings. Once you decide to move into the action steps of signing a purchase agreement and a new loan, or move up to your first large multi-family or be involved in your first REIT, you may want to consider the network of people you have met and decide if a mentorship would be a good fit for you.

A mentor offers you the ability to learn from and with another while actually moving forward with the transaction. This will help make your growth a reality. Sometimes people generalize and assume that mentors are only used by someone new to the field.

Mentorship in business, if used correctly, should be redefined many times along your career path. It is generally a good time to reestablish a new mentor relationship as you are moving up to the next level in your goals, switching paths with investment types, or possibly changing the location of investment properties.

Remember that most seasoned investors are very busy so you need to be very clear upfront how this relationship will also benefit them. There are so many different sizes and sources for this mentorship role that I can only suggest you really spend time exploring your options. I have learned a wealth of information from various mentors in many different capacities for both starting my business and investing.

When my business first started, we were fortunate enough to be selected to be a part of an AMEX OPEN ASK project Hosted at Kellogg School of Management in Chicago by Dr. Saras. This full day kick-off proceeded a year of follow up with each company to learn the techniques needed to seek out help from successful figures in your industry. The program included roleplaying and the added value of revealing previous success stories of people who were continuing the practice of the formula.

I have always implemented the philosophy that asking another thought leader for their help has always been beneficial. The most important takeaway is to always be giving your help in the spirit of paying it forward. Most successful people in the real estate industry are extremely willing to help you with your challenges. Real estate is an ever-changing game and because of this, I am happy to provide mentorship to investors in my REIA groups, clients, or friends seeking guidance.

Many times, members are presented with challenges and I am happy to provide ideas or names of people who might be able to assist them, from government leaders to other board members. The value of getting involved cannot be stressed enough. The benefit of sharing best practices is that it can only add to your resources. A good example of that is the renewal process. The renewal process involves a carefully timed event so the many dates and tasks involved can be daunting. By sharing how to implement a multi-touch, multi-step process, the new landlord can learn to save thousands of dollars.

Clearly, short-term and long-term mentorship provides a stabilizing force in many transitions you will encounter during your growth. The more determined you are to explode your real estate investment portfolio, the more significant this role becomes. A mentor helps you move forward to transform flat, one-sided education into the reality of the bumps and bruises that come with action.

This relationship should give you a feeling of empowerment. You want to feel comfortable with the advice and experience and be able to question the areas that may not be in full alignment with your specific scenario. It's generally before you select a mentor, whether in a networking group, real estate association, or in your business travels, that you should ask yourself some significant questions. Does this person share experiences that most closely align with my goals, ethics, and my specific market? Have they had meaningful experience with my niche, whether that is single-family, multi-family, buy and hold, or fix and flip? A meaningful experience may mean not necessarily that they are extremely successful, but that they certainly live the values and have achieved a level of experience through previous success or failures that will benefit your learning curve.

I once heard it summarized similar to this: The most successful industry leaders will be resilient in the face of challenges and discover resourceful ways to overcome their obstacles. They will be on top of industry trends. They will have a deep and clear vision about where they are going, how they are getting there, and who's going with them.

CHAPTER 12

# Building your team

Building a winning real estate investment team is an ongoing project. The many people needed and the human cycle of life will dictate that change is a constant in your team. And you will certainly learn to value the short stretches with no new learning curves or team members. The human roles of the team scenario illustrate the need to document your process as tightly as possible so when change occurs, you can quickly place a new team member.

Lists, lists, and more lists will help you build that winning team. For example, having a list of tasks that are involved each month in the management of your tenants ensures that if someone is out for the week, another team member should be able to reference the tasks. With that in mind, we put together a table to help you decide on some on the foundational roles in your journey.

You may be entering the next phase of investing or just starting, but either way, this list should be a reminder of the relationships you'll need with that new opportunity in that new city. Keep in mind that interviewing for these roles requires a great deal of time. Shortcutting that process through your involvement in professional organizations and trade shows will help boost the value of your memberships.

Just as real estate agents cannot list a house, perform repairs, inspect, and secure financing for a potential buyer, you cannot perform all the tasks needed to guarantee your success. Every person in the chain has a specific purpose.

Your motivation may blind you to the fact that there are not enough hours in your day to get everything you want done. Regardless of your background, start by selecting team members who are full of energy and passion and share your vision. Some investors provide goals and incentives to contractors to earn an extra edge of loyalty.

When you learn to diversify, you delegate the authority to other people who join your team. You are not transferring control, but you are trusting someone to finish a task just as well as you would yourself. You should set milestones to check their progress and re-evaluate as needed. Consider the value of outsourcing your day-to-day routine, including administrative tasks such as preparing leases, collecting money, and handling renewals. Outsourcing these roles guarantees you can quickly terminate a relationship that is not providing you value compared to hiring a staff member. It also alleviates your risks involved with unemployment charges and additional insurance and office costs. Do a thorough job of checking references no matter which role you are hiring for.

When I work with a client to secure a new team member, I have a list of questions prepared that identifies the likelihood of the vendor empathizing with our goals. Ensuring empathy means this vendor understands or has experienced the unique struggles of the real estate investment industry.

For example, a contractor who has only worked on single-family homeowner rehab projects does not understand the holding costs associated with a delay in their work and might not value the priority of juggling his other projects to meet our deadline date. Too many vendors, contractors, and professionals assume that the "other guy" has the good life and they do not honor their agreement to the highest standard or provide the value as originally agreed. Using an open dialogue to ask questions that describe relevant scenarios and concerns can help identify any warning signs during the selection process.

How do we evaluate a contractor's passion for their skill set? It might start with an open-ended question about the project they remember most that perhaps caused them to work the most hours beyond their normal day. Have them describe that project and how they felt when it was completed.

I can think of several projects that I worked on through the night or certainly close to it, and in all those cases I was more passionate and fired up than when I started. Difficult challenges can provide us with a sense of pride when we conquer them. Contractors of any kind will not take kindly to being dumped on and abused with poor planning. Those are not the passionate projects they will describe. But if they describe for you where they achieved a success with a large goal, a rehab, a flip, or negotiating with a tenant – stories in which they played a key role in delivering the outcome most desired by their client – you will start to sense a good match. Starting with questions like these should give you great insight in order to make an informed decision.

| Role | Name | Email | Mobile/Text |
|------|------|-------|-------------|
| Your mentor | | | |
| Real Estate Agent | | | |
| Real Estate Agent | | | |
| Mortgage Broker | | | |
| Mortgage Broker | | | |
| Hard Money Lender | | | |
| Private Lender | | | |
| Title Office | | | |
| Real Estate Attorney | | | |
| Appraiser | | | |
| Banking Relationship | | | |
| Accountant | | | |
| Bookkeeper | | | |
| Insurance Agent | | | |
| General Handyman | | | |
| General Handyman | | | |
| Cleaning Team | | | |
| General Contractor (s) | | | |
| Electrical Contractor | | | |
| Electrical Contractor | | | |
| Plumbing Contractor | | | |
| Plumbing Contractor | | | |
| HVAC Contractor | | | |
| HVAC Contractor | | | |
| Flooring Contractor | | | |
| Flooring Contractor | | | |
| City Inspector | | | |
| Property Management | | | |
| Virtual Landlord Helper | | | |
| Leasing Agent | | | |

CHAPTER 13

# The Three Pillars That Help You Move Forward and Double Your Growth

## PASSION

The first pillar is passion. I used definitions from Merriam-Webster and chose a couple that I thought were most related for this unit and how you can move forward. Passion is "a strong feeling of enthusiasm or excitement for something or about doing something." It "is an intense, driving or overmastering feeling or conviction, a strong liking or desire for, or devotion to some activity, object or concept."

Most real-estate-related small businesses start out with this passion and conviction for the owner's dream. There are all-night sessions involved, real estate meetings, and more to acquire a particular property. They are trying to meet a common goal, and that common goal drives all of the people who are involved.

This could be as concentrated as a husband and wife driving around looking for properties, or it could be a group of partners also searching for properties. The same could be said when they're putting in the offers. Those often involve all-night sessions as they try to research just what will the cost be. It might mean multiple phone calls to vendors. It's almost an adrenaline-driven activity that involves everybody putting their best efforts in, because remember, it's a time-sensitive activity.

When you talk about passion and taking your business to the next level, you see that as you begin to acquire property, it becomes harder and harder to find the time to put into these tasks to keep up that level of passion and commitment. When you start a company's task, you start to see the vision. When you start to grow that company, it's important that the client's tone and new level of customer service is defined. In other words, it becomes the culture of how they want their residents to feel when they're in their property.

One of the things that we always suggest when working with somebody who is looking to outsource activities, be it with full property management or partially outsourced, is to hone in on the ability to listen to what that vendor can provide for them and make sure that the stories they share and the experience other clients have had of them indicate that they can match that tone and the level of commitment that they're setting for their company.

The company's vision often includes their values and the different language that they believe in using. For instance, some people refer to occupants as "tenants," while others have a strict policy that they are referred to only as a "resident." You see the latter particularly with a class A property.

As you grow, you want to make sure that if you're hiring internal employees that they maintain your sense of your passion and that they're going to match your values, your beliefs, and your vision. You'll want to make sure that you're reviewing their past accomplishments and you're looking for an overall pattern that's going to match what your vision is. Along with sharing that passion, you're providing clarity of purpose about the environment. You want to be sure that each employee understands that they're going to be expected to put their heart into it and again, whatever your level of passion is you'll share. You'll collaborate.

## PEOPLE

There's a famous quote that states, "Surround yourself with the right five people and you'll find that you'll always succeed." And my dad, one of the wisest people I knew, used to say, "You want to be with winners, not losers." Not surprisingly, one of the pillars relates to people. This pillar is about how integral it is to identify the right people for your success.

Another famous quote I hear a lot is, "Hire slowly and fire quickly." When speaking to a potential new employee or vendor, follow your gut. If something doesn't feel right, you don't want to move forward.

To hone in on the best people, you must determine the type of workers who are going to fit your business model. In addition to passion and compatible core values, you should also clearly define what a potential team member's growth plan is. You had your growth plan and now they need theirs. See how these fit together?

When we talk about a growth plan, sometimes people kind of get anxious, but a growth plan could be something you draw on a white board. It could be something that you've done on a yellow pad, but it's got to be that document that you're going to hold yourself to and share with the employees. Whether you're working with a coach and accountability partner or not, that growth plan becomes a fundamental document for finding the right people.

One example we talk about when it comes to people is how some people will outsource to websites such as Fiverr to find talent for project-based activities. Even in a project-based world, when you go to those sites, like with anything today when it's Internet related, you don't get a result of one, but thousands.

When seeking help, instead of you putting your work out there to bid, I would say do the reverse. You do your homework and read about those people and what they've done, who they've done it for, look at their reviews and only then would I approach them and send out a bid.

Once you've narrowed it down to five people, then you can specifically just write to those five people and say, "How much would this project be?" as opposed to you just putting out the project. You'll get hit by a hundred or more replies and some may or may not have any skill level for what you need. Pre-vet those people by reading through their existing reviews. This is no different than somebody who is not sure which restaurant to go to who now opens up Yelp and reads those reviews first. It is also no different than Amazon where people are counting on those reviews prior to purchasing a book.

Have a clear picture to share of your strengths and weaknesses, what opportunities you'll offer, a vision of where you see your company in the next three to five years. Then pose the same questions of the person who you might be taking on, or the company that you might be working with. Finding that out helps you to not only find the right people, but also to help you evaluate what opportunities you'll have with them and what risks are going to be involved in their role. Keep in mind that especially with a small business like real estate investors, you're not necessarily attracting people who are looking for a job with full benefits and such, so you really want to be careful that you're finding a person or company who can provide you with that flexibility.

What are more resources you can use to find these people? A social media post is a great option. Craigslist has a gig portion that's free so you can advertise for help with a specific project.

Going to an REIA meeting provides unique opportunity, even with lenders, to informally interview those people because you're in a setting where you're just having a casual conversation. You're building a relationship with them first before deciding, based on that relationship, to make an appointment to move forward with using them in a specific line of work.

Recently, at one of our local REIA meetings, we had what we refer to as a lender panel. I received feedback from the follow-up meetings that two or three of the lenders in the panel were used just based on how they presented themselves. Being in those informal settings provides a wonderful opportunity.

An event for the Chicagoland's Condo Co-op and Apartment Expo was recently held and it drew over 300 different vendors. This is a great situation to surround yourself with industry experts and gather a large amount of information at once. Now that's a little bit more of a trade show environment, so interaction will happen more with people at booths, but it still provides a great opportunity to educate yourself and make connections.

## PROCESS

So far, we've talked about establishing your passion and having the right people. The last pillar, process, ties the first two together. Process, as defined by

Merriam-Webster, is a series of actions that produce something or lead to a particular result.

With the vision and people in place, we can then determine what recurring tasks can be turned into a process. What we're looking for there is to take those tasks and combine them into things that can be now repeatable and scalable. We go through those tasks and prioritize and categorize them. This can also be defined as automation.

Let's use an example of something as simple as a reminder to pay rent. Let's say that there's a landlord who knocks on each door on the first of the month to collect rent. Another may opt to mail a notice. Another landlord may utilize text or email. The point is, this is a task that can be refined through process and support from the other pillars to save you time and makes your business more efficient. Whether you decide to go door to door or text, your process needs to be identified.

One of the exercises you could go through in this particular unit after you've determined your passions would be to identify your task list. Set those goals and help the people involved re-prioritize as you're shifting through your growth stages. Because what may have been important with three employees may no longer be important with 30.

One of the skill sets we often say is important is project management. This is the ability to evaluate all those tasks and set them in a specific order to get them done in the most cost-efficient manner within the defined timeframe and to be able to apply different contractors to different tasks on that list. It is a fantastic and valuable skill in this industry, especially when it comes to rehab efforts.

The difference between project management and any other type of operational management is that with project management you're always working with a set time. For example, I just read about a company that always works on an eight-week cycle. Rather than define what specific features will make it in a particular new release of their product, they instead work within a timeline because their project management theory warns against this: Work expands to fill in the time. If you give somebody six months, you don't necessarily have a better-developed product. This way, you work on specific things in small bites and move on to the next after eight weeks.

This approach is very interesting in terms of growing your portfolio because you should be setting time-based goals, i.e. by month, quarter, and annually. Take a look at that task list and shift the priorities, the people, and the process. It helps you learn and understand this critical path, which is the factor that drives that date. From there you can determine what tasks can be aligned to that and what tasks must be done in a specific order.

For instance, the testing of a software product cannot be done until the software is done, so until that eight-week period is up, you're waiting. You must be sure that everything is set in order. There are always areas in our process where we're going to experience bottlenecks; where there's not enough resources to assign to that, thus causing this deadline.

We want to avoid those whenever possible so that work is flowing and the process is smooth, so sitting down and itemizing is key. Look for items that require the same skill set. That might help you decide what can be outsourced. If there's x number of bookkeeping tasks involved with the collection of rent, then maybe that's something you can outsource because all these tasks are related.

One of the things that we always suggest is a technology solution, as it will streamline and help you reduce your margin for errors. For instance, an employee is posting your payments at the end of the day to each ledger. There's a human element to that. Correct? A person could make mathematical errors, but a program has a reconciliation feature. Some big companies might make three deposits per day. Smaller ones may not go every day, so the point is there's a technology solution that will help evaluate that process and reduce those margins of error for businesses of any size.

Customer Relationship Management Software (CRM) helps you develop a relationship with your contacts. CRM software is generally what you see most often used when you're trying to solicit someone for a particular position or to buy from your company. It will keep all the specific dates and times, so you'll be able to sort and track down to the last detail. And again, there is a reduced margin of error. Salesforce is a very popular tool utilized by small businesses and corporations alike. There are also platforms specific to property management.

All those different technology solutions allow you to analyze that data quicker to make a good decision. A lot of landlords and real estate investors look to CRM solutions to keep track of the many vendors they interface with so they have a comprehensive list of contractors, vendors, and banks. Maybe they have people at the auction houses, so maintaining a database of those in something like a CRM software can be very helpful.

In our current real estate market, which cycles, of course, contractors can be extremely busy. For this and other obvious reasons, you want to be as specific as possible with your task request. In order to have a successful relationship with those contractors, you must have what they would refer to as a clear scope of work. This should include a very clear outline of each task and the associated processes.

The shape of the housing market doesn't necessarily matter, but you need to realize that depending on where we are in a cycle, it can be harder to find contractors who are willing to spend time with you to physically walk through a building. They want you to at least be able to send over that list of tasks so they can provide their rough draft. Then they will usually provide you with a bid, contingent on unexpected restraints when they see the property in person.

You want to make sure your process is as tight as can be. There are times that you can miss a deadline by a day or two days. Obviously, having delays is part of a process. But taking the time to define it as clearly as possible in all areas will mitigate much of the risk.

Take an auction, for example. Once a property goes on to auction, you've got to be prepared to bring a cashier's check to the property if you want it. In order to have the money readily available to put down for the home, you must have your ducks in a row with all other aspects of your business to know that the money is truly available to spend. The more that you can define the process involved with purchasing an auction property, the more you develop and sharpen your ability to do related tasks such as rough estimates.

One of the tips that I would give people if they were just starting, especially with an auction property that's up through foreclosure or a sheriff sale (anything that's very time sensitive), is to take the time to go through the process with an experienced landlord. There are lot of people who are more than willing to share what they know, and you can offer them some value in return. Maybe you can use your computer skills and do something for them that will save them time. What you'd be doing is trading off a skill set you have for that owner, in order for them to aid you in doing the background work to start to develop your list of processes.

Taking the time to find a mentor who you're able to offer some value to, and then witnessing and being a part of their process, really helps you reduce your learning curve and make a more accurate assessment of that free template. While there is plenty of potentially helpful information on the Internet, I highly recommend the route of investing the time to find and work with a mentor. It will set your investment career off on a much stronger path!

Let's dig into a specific and very important process for landlords: rent collection. This process comes with its own built-in timeline. Based on your lease, if the rent is due on the first, if it has a five-day grace period, then it's late on the sixth. If that happens, then a legal document needs to go out. A legal document requires X number of days before you can take it to court. For instance, five business days after they were served you can go ahead to court. If you are in one of those situations, that timeline and that process is key. Do you have to take it to court on the sixth day? No, but the point is, you have that timeline. You have that visual. You understand what time of the month it is, where you should be in that process, and just what your next steps are. That's a simple example, but the same can be true with a rehab project, knowing which task and how many days are allocated for each task. Those sets of processes aid in estimating and then comparing your estimate against the actual, which can also better inform you for future projects.

In project management, I talk about the "post" phase of project management. There really needs to be a post wrap-up once you've delivered that product so that you can see where your estimates were wrong. You may have also learned that certain vendors are incapable of performing certain duties in X number of days, so you'll have to revise that number or replace your vendor. These are lessons learned, something you'll want to capture at the end of each project.

It may seem as though there are so many tasks that it will inhibit you from growing. But this is exactly why the outsourcing exists. Rather than being unaware of what needs to be done, you'll have a clear picture and can delegate any tasks that can be better served by someone else.

We covered a lot in this chapter, so here are the key takeaways:

- Establish your passion, people, and process and continually revisit them
- Let your software do the heavy lifting whenever possible.
- Automating where you can is going to reduce time and the element of human error, thus reducing the number of areas where money can leak out.
- Focusing your efforts allows you to seek out and solve more problems and zone in on opportunity.

Make sure you have big goals for yourself. What's the next level you can take your portfolio to? How can you take it there? Dig deep and keep these pillars in mind and you'll change your future!

# CHAPTER 14

# Adding Value

Anyone who has worked with a marketing consultant when starting up their business knows that most often, the first task is to help you develop a statement of your unique value proposition. Simply defined, value is about offering your clients a service that they give a higher significance to, over and above what the expected fees are. As a consumer, you may value the quality of a service and be willing to pay more if you feel the value enriches and enhances both your needs and wants.

Secure Pay One provides a unique value to our clients as we supplement investors' staff with the latest in ever-evolving technology resources and a professional staff that prioritizes their portfolio growth. We provide an exceptional service that walks the fine line of enforcing their lease agreements while providing their residents the on-demand service hours and quick replies our society has come to expect. We strive to offer all the latest in payment methods and options to ensure the flexibility needed to establish a cash flow. In summary, we listen to the needs of each client and provide real estate investors with the best possible and timely service. This ensures peace of mind for us, knowing we are always available to help our clients in the many challenging roles they may face on a daily basis.

Your unique value proposition is the driving force behind the significance of your business. If you entered the business to get rich quickly, you have probably figured out by now that you entered the wrong business. If you entered real estate to reduce the hours from your full-time job you are probably in the wrong business.

Truth be told, a successful business takes hard work and an exceptional commitment to excellence. You are in the people business and people like to do business with good people. You must examine and identify early on that the tenant is your client, so providing them with exceptional service will serve your company's best interest.

Each tenant paying rent at $1,000 represents a $12,000 annual fundamental line item in your budget. Therefore, understanding your client is a driving force for every business and buy and hold rentals are no different. When you screen for a tenant, I would suggest you treat the application as a business relationship and achieve a clear understanding from both sides of what the prerequisites are to maintain mutually beneficial long-term goals.

Consider implementing a resident monthly e-newsletter that focuses on the expectations you have of a safe and healthy home and to serve as a reminder of current activities in your area. The newsletter provides you, the landlord, with an opportunity to remind your tenant of timely rent payments and seasonal inspections.

Adding value shouldn't stop with the resident. Watch for opportunities to add value with the many vendors who are part of your team. You can help your vendors learn best business practices.

We have worked with successful real estate investors who take the time to invite vendors in for free business classes. Some even offer them networking dinners to meet with other vendors and clients who can refer their services. Hosting networking events and educational opportunities for your vendors lets them know how much they mean to the overall success of your business. Value their time and avoid imposing unrealistic, constricted deadlines caused by poor planning. Respecting the vendor's significance to your success will set up a good foundation of mutual respect and you will find them impressing you with their ability to turn over requests in a tight timeframe.

Once identified, develop the talent of your vendors and team. When your business is set up with a process they will be able to reduce your workload by sharing a process that equally saves you money and time. I, for example, have clients who create easily updated templates for personal financial statements so they can quickly be brought up to date with changes. Having all loan documents readily assessable provides value to their mortgage lender. On the flip side, the lender is more than willing to put in the extra hours it takes to get a loan package submitted and approved in a short timeframe knowing how well organized the landlord is.

We enrich some of our client relationships by providing clarity to the scope and details needed of the work. We assemble packets and scan and distribute information to their residents and vendors via email or U.S. mail. We can work directly with their legal team to reduce legal fees by keeping up with timely documentation. And one of the most prevalent areas that we assist with is the renewal process. Working with an owner to develop a master list of tasks can reduce vacancy days that may lead to a substantial loss of income.

As My Landlord Helper, we essentially do, or at least offer, it all. Utilizing a similar service, plus selecting a talented and trustworthy team equals both tangible and intangible value to an investor. You'll free up time to focus on what most needs your attention – the bottom line.

CHAPTER 15

# **REIA**

The letters REIA simply stand for the Real Estate Investment Association, but it does not simply stops there. An REIA may be a not-for-profit or a for-profit association. The National REIA can be used as a source for locating an REIA in your area. Their website, nationalreia.org, boldly boasts "promote, protect, and educate." You can do a web search to find a local REIA in your town. It is important to note, though, that each REIA has an individual mission statement and underlying tone to the organization. Selecting an REIA involves multiple meetings to gain a clear understanding of what symmetry you can align with in the group.

I am currently the President of an REIA in Lake County, Illinois and I keep active with over seven local REIAs as well as two national REIAs. The education I receive by listening to the speakers and the issues of others far exceeds the time I put into the meetings. These learnings and takeaways will catapult you as grow your portfolio.

Many investors use the REIA as a great place to find and locate partners for their business. The Lake County Property Investors Association (LCPIA) is a not-for-profit that has provided networking and education for over 25 years. The founding members of our group conveyed a strong vision and followed up with by-laws to ensure future boards carry on the mission. We value relationships first, and relationships that are made in our REIA span from months to years.

I personally have developed strong relationships with many industry thought leaders in both local and national REIAs. I have met local housing representatives, judges, lawyers, and county officials who are always willing to give advice when I have a challenge.

These relationships provide the foundation or the first level of education. We learn by sharing experiences and band together when laws are proposed that are unfair to real estate investors. Attending REIA meetings provides valuable opportunities for you to cultivate the relationships to build your team members. It is often said that we purchase from people who we know, like, and trust, and certainly your real estate business will be no different. Attending the meetings on a regular basis will provide you with the depth of insight to vet out the sincerity of the vendors as well as their level of commitment. You can add many contacts to your resource tool belt to face the many challenges that lie in the real estate investment business. The education at REIA meetings will most often include main speakers for topics specific to real estate investment properties. You should expect to meet local governmental officials ranging from the real estate tax assessment office to the sheriff's office. You will find topics on property management software as well as valued input from real estate accountants and lawyers.

By volunteering, you can become part of the solution to issues that the group may need to address. If you are in a large metro area, consider joining more than one REIA to increase your networking and to expose yourself to many philosophies, speakers, and networking options. While you learn about topics like wholesaling, MLS listings, and postcard campaigns, speakers will present opportunities for you to grow.

CHAPTER 16

# Organizing for the Shift

Experts are warning that the real estate industry has just begun another shift. It's too soon to tell the impact on our investors, but the stock of low-priced homes has tightened some and deal hunting is a bit more difficult. Once clarified, this will result in a tightening market for the appetite of the majority of our investors.

Most savvy investors look to purchase at low, low prices and the scarcity will result in fewer deals. During these times, they will continue to look at creative ways to structure new purchases. As with most market cycles, it will be a great time to take a moment to reflect on expenses and other areas of their business. Many times, the clients who call us and schedule a strategy meeting have us assist with reviewing agreements and their process.

I always suggest that investors review goals daily, spending 30 minutes searching for properties and checking fundamentals. If they are monitoring daily over a 30- or 60- or 90-day period, they will identify changing conditions in their local market. Following the data enables you to develop a deep personal understanding of your market and apply your human analysis tool, intuition, to a market you study consistently.

Investors should always look for areas to reduce expenses associated with vendors or current arrangement and should review this with their full-service property manager. Our friend Matt in California feels strongly that the most money lost on a regular basis can be attributed to a bad property management team. The way Matt explains it is that the investor and manager's business model may not be aligned. Depending on how the agreement is structured, your manager may get paid a fee whenever a new tenant is brought in to begin a new lease on your property, resulting in improper screening and no worries when a tenant defaults resulting in eviction and lost rent. But oh, wait! The manager will be happy to find a replacement tenant for their usual fee of one month's rent.

Using a property manager can be an expense. Investors may analyze the worth of this as there is more pressure to reduce costs when the real estate market tightens, but this can be especially evident at times when you are not happy with the manager's performance.

This is in direct contrast to the investor who is working very hard to keep turnover at a minimum and would like to add incentives to attract long-term tenants. We often help investors determine an incentive-based program that supports a resident's ability to feel valuable. We also help organize simple acts with coupon blasts from the area and emails with local events.

As the market shifts with purchasing, so do rental shifts. Some of you may remember when vacancies spiked and each landlord began offering incentives such as the first month free and potentially also free Internet and cable. As we move into 2017, developing a stand-by list of low-cost incentives will be key for both new tenants and retention. Know your market and your numbers. Collecting the majority of rents as listed in your income projections vs. lingering vacancies can certainly represent a major shift to the balance sheet.

Shifting markets require you to always be planning and documenting ideas for your Plan B. They require you to review your portfolio now and diversify where possible. Diversity of building type and location ensures that if something changes in one part of your portfolio, you are well prepared. Identifying areas of the country where you see increased investment in infrastructure and job markets are all part of emerging trends.

## CREATIVE REWARDS PROGRAM

Implementing your creative rewards program in a shifting market models your incentives to the loyalty programs offered by the big box stores. Rather than implement ideas the tenants might not like or something that doesn't mean much to them, however, consider a rewards renewal menu at their lease anniversary date. The menu should have one-year, two-year, and five-year options, which visually reminds your residents annually that long-term residents are appreciated and rewarded.

While gift cards and cash reductions are popular to some people, let your tenants select what they'd prefer. If a new rent amount has been proposed, be open to negotiating if the tenant reaches out to you. Also, it is always helpful to include a physical gift which serves as a nice visual reminder. New small but bright LED flashlights are handy for autos and are convenient to carry along in a bag or when walking.

Consider adding items on the renewal menu that a tenant wouldn't normally buy for themselves. We suggest you attempt to keep a stock of electronics when they are offered at seasonally low prices. Consider purchases such as inexpensive large screen televisions, tablets, and small electronics. The cost of small gifts will be well worth it to keep premier tenants for another year.

Financial incentives also provide an appeal to most people, so consider providing your tenant the option to reduce expenses as a menu option for renewal.

Some ideas include a coupon to reduce the rent that can be applied to one-time payments or a coupon for cleaning services the resident might use when hosting a special event. In extremely tight markets you may also offer a free month of rent, a lease renewal cash bonus, or a credit for a utility. When tenants are shopping around, they will be happy to know that a renewal menu might provide the best deal.

Property improvements might include any upgrade that is permanent to the unit. Many of our landlords include new paint, new flooring, or carpet cleaning, while some consider upgraded appliance options or new blinds for one window. If your rental property is furnished, consider new furniture that will stay put when the tenant eventually moves out. Property upgrades of all types increase your investment's worth and tenants can benefit from small changes that give them the feel of a new and upgraded surrounding.

Following the lead of some commercial landlords, a worthwhile incentive can include a "build-out option" to customize the space.

You can add custom shelving to closets, which in turn remain an upgrade to your unit. Most tenants love the thought of additional closet shelving or a reorganized storage space.

Don't forget that this renewal menu will not be an increased expense but instead a savings of turnover, vacancy, or an expense – realize you have not lost funds to reduced rent and additional vacancy days.

Remember replacing a good tenant can be very costly, so consider these options for anniversary renewals as a thank you for valued residents:

- Clean carpets
- Install new flooring in one room
- Upgrade or replace an appliance
- Preferred tenant parking stall (if available)
- Paint a room
- Install a ceiling fan
- Flat screen TV
- Google Home/Amazon Alexa
- Sports tickets
- Annual pass to an amusement park
- Furniture
- Hotel getaway
- Reduce rent
- Offer a free last month rent (with history of no late payments)
- Pay one or more utilities for a month
- Renewal bonus gift card
- Bonus for two qualified referrals
- Coupons and certificates for local eateries

# CHAPTER 17

# Identifying and Learning from Top DIY Landlord Mistakes

As we started in the business of helping landlords, it became clear that we needed to assist our clients while expanding our communications. So, we began to initiate a best practices collection. Too many times we were witnessing a common thread amongst new clients and we felt compelled to share and help reduce the learning curve. As a landlord comes to My Landlord Helper eager to scale their business, it becomes a foundational exercise to begin with identifying tasks that may inhibit growth. There is a clear benefit in learning top mistakes that other landlords consider to be "huuuge" as The Donald would describe.

Of course, the conversation most often starts with establishing a business approach to your rentals. So many times, landlords are surprised to hear this and many have not consulted an attorney or accountant to properly set up a title and LLC to protect their asset and their family. While at the beginning money might have been tight, it is essential that at the minimum you discuss what risks you are exposed to when leaving the property in your name, and thus the lease directly in your individual name.

My first client, John B., left his property in his own name for two years and then began the slow process of protecting his assets and his family with some good legal counsel on what worked best in his individual scenario. His attorney advised on using a series of individual LLCs. While I realize that legal fees stack quickly, I think it is an essential step in reducing risks and maximizing the legal and tax benefits property investments offer you. Keep in mind that as you grow and your family evolves and morphs, this is another good time to restructure as needed.

## #1 SCREEN YOUR TENANTS

Tenant screening is perhaps the most important thing a landlord can do. Don't "fall in love" with the personality of your candidate. The most important first step is to get to know each other by sharing small talk and rapport, discussing any line items on the credit report. The next part of the process is to validate the small talk with follow up calls or emails.

## #2 TREAT RENTALS AS A BUSINESS

A big mistake is not allocating one account for your business, losing receipts, and generally keep things unorganized. Landlording is not a hobby. If you want to make money you must treat landlording as a business and categorize all your expenses.

## #3 BENDING POLICY FOR THE STORY

The first few times some of your tenants may be late they will share with you the life event triggering the issue. It is the ruin of many competent entrepreneurs and real estate investors when they let their heart make the financial business decisions. The analytical spreadsheets you used to purchase the property and analyze the cash flow will not change. If you enter into short-term loans, you may end up turning the formula around and risk losing the building. Professionals assist their tenant in finding outside resources and charitable organizations that offer funding specifically to help in short-term situations. A life event that changes the tenant's finances must be handled professionally to review if the income formula used to qualify them for the unit is still valid. Think about this. Will your bank or lender let *you* slide?

# #4 GET EVERYTHING IN WRITING AND ADD PICTURES

Be sure dates, times, repairs, and upgrades are listed or omitted on a checklist. Many times, we see DIY landlords try to be nice and promise items that meant a small expense and the tenant hold a completely different expectation. Do not promise items and communicate in writing via text or image on issues that may be vague.

# #5 UNDERSTAND THE COST OF BUSINESS AND REPAIRS

Have a clear list of the cost of doing repairs. Call other landlords or seek advice from an REIA. Develop the top ten items that most commonly break and develop and estimate matrix of the average time to fix them with the hourly rate. Keep this available for your records and share it with your tenants as issues arise.

# #6 KNOW THE LAW

There are laws that are specific to your municipality, your county, and your state. It is your job as a landlord to be aware of them. For example, what are the legal steps needed to evict a non-paying tenant? It is sobering to learn that DIY landlords are not aware of these laws in their town. Gone are the days of taking off doors when no rent has been paid. It is very important to do your best to avoid and discuss non-payment issues but also know the tenant is not your friend. Violating laws through inexperience can be very expensive if the case ends up in court.

# #7 SKIPPING PROPERTY INSPECTIONS

It is to your advantage to proactively schedule filter checks, seasonal cleaning, or other inspections that provide you with a report card of the condition of the property.

Successful landlords know that they need to stay competitive and to have a clear understanding of the business. Identify areas with the highest potential for risk and implement solutions to reduce that risk. While each market is unique, a DIY landlord needs to learn techniques that will improve their ability to run their business profitably. As a small business owner, you need to constantly watch market trends and make improvements to escalate your options for success.

# CHAPTER 18

# Shopping for the Best "Landlord Helper" for You

We touched on the importance of seeking help in managing your properties earlier, but in this chapter, we will dive deeper. An investor trying to expand his or her portfolio will eventually need some type of assistance to avoid spending time on current tenants rather than getting on and seeking new investments. What is essential, though, is to determine what type of "help" is best for you. Turning your portfolio over to a full property management company that may not always have your best interest in mind and is not always conscious of your budget may not be the right fit for you.

Although it is difficult to picture giving up a percentage of your tenant's rent each month to a management company, it is important to consider that managing your properties independently can be a full-time job. As you begin to grow your portfolio, you will start to see the amount of time it takes to handle collection, answer maintenance calls, coordinate repairs, initiate the renewal process, and many other aspects that come along with renting your properties. As an investor, you want your job to be seeking new ventures and landing new deals – not answering toilet calls.

Another important aspect of utilizing some type of assistance in managing your properties is the ability to establish someone who is between the owner and the tenant. In this case, the owner can maintain a sense of anonymity. The tenant's main form of communication is your "landlord helper," therefore they do not have the ability to come to you, the owner, and ask for an extension on rent or provide an excuse for being late.

As opposed to utilizing full property management, many consider hiring an employee or two to work in the office and assist with calls, payments, and other documents. Though this may seem like a better option than full property management, there are many reasons why I would encourage you to explore the benefits of using a company over an employee. A company that can assist you in managing your properties while you remain in control of decisions may be the option to consider. A company that can take calls, handle collections, coordinate maintenance, etc. can be hired or fired at any time. If you hire an employee who doesn't work out, you may be forced into paying unemployment. If the company you choose doesn't work out, you can be done with them when you choose.

After landing on the decision that you do want to seek a landlord helper, you now have the challenge of determining what to look for in one. A helpful tool when shopping for your landlord helper is to create a table or matrix that includes all the potential companies you want to call or meet with, along with all the things you are looking for in a company. As you make your calls, using this tool will ensure that you are asking all the right questions each time and will assist you in comparing one company against another.

Develop a matrix to use when seeking a management company for assistance.

- How many properties do they manage?
- How many payment options do they offer?
- What is their fee structure?
- Are there additional fees that may be charged? Are they listed in the agreement?
- What is the cancellation clause?
- Do fees vary based on vacancy?
- What are the leasing fees?
- What marketing styles do you use that are unusual?
- What standards do you use in selecting a new tenant?

- What control do I have on input to the lease agreement?
- Do you have a suggested timeline of inspections?
- Will I have real time availability of my reports?
- Do they charge additional fees?
- How will they help with renewals, when the unit is empty, etc.

Another important question to consider when choosing a company is their communication style. How often will they communicate with you? Are you looking for a company that will take over all aspects of your properties without informing you of decisions made, or would you rather stay informed and have input?

The renewal process can be challenging is well. Will a property management company be conscious of your turnover rate or whom they fill your unit with? Some property management companies only issue increases when a new tenant moves in, rather than when a current tenant renews. Will the company assist with increases each year to help you get more money from your investment?

Although ideally we hope that we will not have to evict any tenants, ending up in situations with a non-paying tenant does occur and in this case it is essential that the eviction process is handled seamlessly. In seeking assistance with your investment properties, you want to be sure you select someone who can assist with this. What is their process for creating legal notices?

In addition to verifying that a company has the things you are looking for, there steps you can take to confirm that you are making the right choice. It is important to review the references provided by each company and determine if they align with your own portfolio. Calling vendors who have worked with specific companies can also be helpful; they may be able to provide an unbiased review of the company.

Finally, any reputable company will have a positive reputation with the Better Business Bureau and other positive online reviews from owners, and when selecting a company it can be helpful to look into this. Most importantly, when selecting a landlord helper, you will want to choose a partner that is prepared to support your business' growth.

CHAPTER 19

# Don't Lose Money
# at Lease Expiration

There is money to be made at the time of the lease renewal. Rents have been rising steadily over the past five years in most areas of the country. Except for some geographic gaps, this has been a national trend with the percentages varying depending on location.

A good renewal process benefits both the resident and the landlord. The savvy real estate investor knows that expenses add up quickly, even on the best turnaround process. Updating the unit, marketing the unit, office resources involved with calls, showing, and potential leasing agent fees are estimated to run anywhere between $500 - $3,500 depending on all the variables. One of the key factors in the renewal process is establishing a strict timeline of dates to ensure vacancy days do not add to this potential loss.

While a tenant is currently living in the unit it is suggested that quarterly inspections take place to ensure it is kept in good working order. Many times, the lease will have language to guarantee that this is communicated upfront, along with a clause that offers incentives to a resident to show the unit in good, clean condition while they are still living in the unit.

The rent management application should be set up to notify you approximately 90 days prior to the lease expiration so a letter or communication can be sent from your office to invite the current tenant to renew. Management and the owner should agree on what the incentive should be. A matrix can be developed that reflects additional compensation for multiple-term tenant renewals. Keep in mind that in addition to not spending money on the unit to modernize the interior at turnover, you may want a gift of dinner or other certificate in lieu of the marketing expense associated with a common one-month leasing agent fee.

## LEASE RENEWAL ANNIVERSARY – THE BENEFITS OF RENEWING YOUR CURRENT TENANT

As the end of your current tenant's lease approaches, you are faced with the difficult task of either renewing the lease or seeking a new tenant. There are many important benefits to renewing the lease of your current tenant instead of going through the headache of getting your unit "rent-ready" all over again, marketing the unit, showing the unit, and screening potential tenants.

In addition to the time and headache you will save, you also stand to save a lot of money by renewing your current lease. If your current tenant does move out, you will need to factor in the cost of paint, cleaning, and any other renovations needed after the current tenant vacates. In addition, there are also costs associated with marketing the unit, screening tenants ($30-$50 for a credit check), one month rent to the broker, and a possible vacancy (loss of one month's rent or more).

Staying on top of your tenant's lease renewal anniversary date is essential to you as a landlord, as it reduces the risk of vacancy. If your current tenant does not renew, it may not be an easy task to locate a responsible tenant and have them lined up to move in the day after your current tenant moves out.

Renewing your current tenant's lease also reduces the risk of obtaining a bad tenant. Rushing to get a new tenant in hopes of not losing a month's rent during the turnover process might result in getting a not-so-stellar candidate in your unit. If your current tenant pays on time, is generally clean, and doesn't cause any damages or disturbances, it is worth the effort of offering them a lease renewal.

The first part, however, is deciding whether you would like to renew your current tenant's lease. If your current tenant is not paying on time or has not been a good tenant and you would like to end the lease, it is important to inform them of this. As the lease end date approaches, you can simply send a letter informing the tenants that their lease expiration date is approaching on a specified date, and you, unfortunately, cannot offer a renewal. Below is an example of a letter you can send out between 60-90 days of approaching expiration date.

*Dear (Tenant's Name),*

*Thank you for staying at "current tenants address." It has been our privilege to serve you and your family's housing needs. At this time, the owner's group is not offering a renewal on your current lease. Please see the attached move-out instructions to have the unit vacated by dd/mm/yyyy (lease end date).*

Sending a letter like this as the end date approaches is important so the tenant is informed that they will need to move out, and will be aware of any showings that might occur in their last few months in the unit.

After deciding that you would like to offer a renewal to your current tenant, there a few things to consider. The first thing to consider is whether you would like to give your tenants an increase. After researching the current rates in the area of your property, you may find that your rent amount may be lower or competitive to surrounding market rents. Offering a small increase can be effective, as it may still be lower or equal to other surrounding prices. Even if the increase brings your rent a little higher than others, tenants find it more convenient and cost effective to renew as opposed to spending money and effort on moving. Below is an example of an increase letter that has served effective to many of our landlords.

*Dear (Tenant's Name),*

*It has been our privilege to serve you and your family's housing needs. We are coming upon your lease renewal anniversary and would like to offer you an incentive to stay in your current home. Current rents in the area have increased between $75-$100, and if you sign and return this form prior to mm/dd, we can offer you an increase of only $25.*

At the bottom of this letter, the tenants can sign off that they agree to the increase and agree to renew until the end date of their new lease.

These letters can also include incentives. If you believe you have good tenants and really do not want the hassle of replacing them, it can be helpful to offer an incentive to stay. Something along the lines of painting a room, replacing or cleaning carpet, or a new microwave or other appliance can be effective. Something as simple as offering a renewal with no increase is an incentive for tenants to stay as market rents at this time continue to climb higher and higher.

The average tenant does not consider their options regarding their lease end until roughly 45 prior to lease expiration. Ideally, you want to begin the renewal process 90 days prior to the lease expiration date. Getting the process started at this point and sending the letter out will ensure that you have an answer 60 days prior to the expiration date. In this case, if the tenant is not renewing, you have time to market and show the unit to ensure you do no miss out on a month of rent. The letter should include a deadline, stating that in order to obtain the offered incentive or lesser increase amount, the tenant must return the form by mm/dd with their decision.

It is also helpful to keep in mind that as much as a tenant move out is inconvenient for you as a landlord, it is equally inconvenient for the tenant. As a helpful landlord, it can be effective to include a move-out checklist and a list of move-out reminders along with the renewal letter, should they decide not to renew. Reviewing this list could potentially persuade them to stay. This list can include:

- Cleaning instruction, or cost of cleaning fees
- Locate moving company: set date and time
- Cancel utilities
- Return keys
- Forward mail
- Notify credit cards, bank, insurance, etc. of new address

Finally, in the event of renewing a lease, depending on your location, you may need to have a new lease signed along with the necessary addendums. Remember to include any disclosures regarding bedbugs, lead paint, and any additional local disclosures that require a signature; they will also need to be signed.

CHAPTER 20

# Setting Up and Remembering Your Goals

When investors first get started in real estate they may set a modest goal to acquire a home and begin to develop cash flow. When they begin investing, they realize that the long game requires that they pay down the mortgage so ultimately, the expense will only be real estate taxes. Once they successfully navigate purchasing and leasing homes or multi-family units, the fever sets in to continue to expand their portfolio.

As with any addiction, the better the investor is at finding off-market-buy low deals, the more properties and bargains they will find. Many times, the investor becomes such a strong name in their local market that their phone rings from wholesalers and banks offering them deals.

Some investors, through bandit signs and letters, may see their work paying back with active calls two or three years down the line.

Long-term visions vary by person. Whatever the goal may be, it is important to establish them and revisit them frequently. My company has made it a practice to regularly review initial strategies and re-evaluate short- and long-term goals. Dependent on their personal situation, if free time is on their radar they may want to find new ways to monetize these opportunities in a more passive attempt. These are important strategy sessions to coach them through implementing some new tactical solutions to best develop the outcome they envision from their real estate investment portfolio.

We also work with investors to outline their annual updated set of standards to measure their success, as well as review a suggested schedule of local REIAs, national conferences, and web-based networking resources. This gives an investor time away from the business to add the clarity needed to review and reframe. Remember that another factor contributing to this annual exercise is the cyclical nature of the real estate property market.

As with any investment, diversification is key to implement as you grow. Investors might evaluate the impact of local geographic strategies to prevent all properties from being hit by a downturn of employment opportunities in one area. Review changes to taxable income and what changes might be needed to the plans. Evaluate opportunities for new partnerships and funding.

We recommend tracking your goals by spending 30 minutes each day evaluating your property goals and 30 minutes to review new property opportunities. Developing a checklist is key, but the next step is to move beyond a task list and begin to prioritize the most important tasks on your calendar. By scheduling the time on your calendar, you ensure that your most important tasks/goals are met by prioritizing the time in your day to accomplish them. This allows you to stay focused and increases your chances of ultimately achieving your established goals by tenfold.

This habit helps you celebrate your achievements and brings you a bigger sense of accomplishment. It also enriches your goal-setting skills, so if your goals are too easily accomplished you will begin to adjust to more challenging goals. Goal setting also allows you to review failures and adjust your skill sets, filling in with education on weaker skill sets.

You may supplement your knowledge with books, QA sections on real estate community websites, and podcasts.

Finally, keep an updated exit strategy and backup plan handy. With goals established, reviewed, and regularly tracked, property investing *can* ultimately help you achieve your goals to create long-term wealth.

# CHAPTER 21

# Setting Up a Strategy Session

When we receive a call from an investor looking to work with us, My Landlord Helper, we send them a profile sheet. This questionnaire helps the investor quickly move through an exercise to find weak areas in their process or areas where we may be able to save them time to expedite their growth. This process helps us determine their strategy for growth and identifies where we can implement the rinse and repeat cycle to their daily/weekly/monthly/annual tasks.

Many times, when an investor starts and is presented with so many great real estate bargains, their portfolio seems to have grown almost unattended. This opportunity allows them to reflect on tasks they'd like to change. Keep in mind, the investor is most pleased knowing the landlord helper will be reporting back to them on winning and losing strategies.

For example, some of our clients clearly identify with the need to bring their systems up to current standards. They need to implement web-based applications for the full rental life cycle, beginning with the application process through move out. The idea is to implement documented repeatable lists and steps that take the knowledge from their head to paper and then automated wherever possible. This session identifies areas where we can significantly make a difference. We counsel them to follow up and brainstorm a long list of tasks that they currently perform and identify areas where they have strengths and why.

The next list can be used to identify areas where small tasks can be outsourced to virtual assistants.

| My Goal Sheet | | | |
|---|---|---|---|
| | Current | 18 months | 36 months |
| How many properties do you manage now? | | | |
| Estimate the breakdown of time spent on your tasks: | | | |
| Marketing | | | |
| Unit showings | | | |
| Unit turnover (rehab make-ready work) | | | |
| Lease signing appointments | | | |
| Payment collections | | | |
| Communication with tenants | | | |
| Payment reminders | | | |
| Follow up calls on payments | | | |
| Preparation of legal notices on late payments | | | |
| Maintenance reminders | | | |
| Performing maintenance follow up | | | |
| Do you currently use a property management web-based application? | | | |
| What current apps are you using to organize your business? | | | |
| Municipality inspections | | | |
| Housing inspections | | | |
| Developing new action plans | | | |
| Researching new properties (auctions, Zillow, MLS, foreclosures, letters) | | | |
| Continuing education seminars | | | |
| Continuing education masterminds | | | |
| Networking and building a team | | | |

How many properties do you currently own or manage?

---

Define your strengths and your goals.

Define areas of the business that are not meeting expectations for your investors.

What systems or processes could you add that will enhance your effectiveness for your clients?

What services or processes can you add that would exceed your client's expectations?

My goals are not getting completed daily and growth is limited because I spend most of my day doing what?
List 5 tasks:

If I could design the perfect day/week/month it would include these tasks...
List 5 tasks:

If I could envision one year from now and my funds were not limited, I would allocate my budget to...
List 5 items you wish you could outsource:

What is the vision for growing your company?

What is limiting that growth?

What are common client misconceptions about your current process?

# Conclusion

Buying and holding real estate property is an ideal way to invest money and grow your wealth. Buying property and growing a portfolio really enables you to be in a position to pass on not just wealth to your family, but also your legacy. It is important to remember that while a real estate portfolio can generate wealth, it is unlikely it would be defined as a true passive income.

I have met so many quality people and found so many valuable resources on my journey. I have witnessed so many mentors willing to share best practices that this book only seemed a natural extension of my need to give back to the real estate investors who will continue on in this space.

By having a deeper understanding of all the pieces that fit into real estate investment, you should now be able to visualize your game plan. In order to boost that portfolio, you have to find some ways to free up time. The fact of the matter is whatever you can automate, automate! The same goes for outsourcing. Find people who share your passion for the industry and for your success and watch for other new technologies penetrating the industry. Doing so will often help you rectify areas where you might be losing money.

When you examine the three pillars, you'll realize that one of the foundational things is setting the right culture and finding the right partners for this journey. People, passion, and process will ultimately guide you ultimately hold yourself accountable to taking the necessary steps to implement the processes that align themselves for your growth.

Equally important is to remember that real estate investment industry is no different than any entrepreneurial journey. It's going to be filled with days of physical, emotional, and unfortunately, sometimes financial pain. So, keeping an open and educated mind is going to be a key step in your growth.

# Bonuses

As a gift to readers, I am offering the following forms for you to implement in your business. Please contact us at Info@SecurePayOne.com to receive them.

1. Sample Management Move-in Checklist template
2. Sample Tenant Information Sheet template
3. Sample Maintenance Fee Schedule template
4. Sample Maintenance Request Form template

Made in the USA
Lexington, KY
20 October 2017